The Amber Forest

Beauty and Biology of California's Submarine Forests

by
**Ronald H. McPeak, Dale A. Glantz
and Carole R. Shaw**

First Printing 1988
Watersport Publishing, Inc., P.O. Box 83727, San Diego, CA 92138

ISBN 0-922769-00-X
ISBN 0-922769-00-1 (pbk.)

Library of Congress Catalog Card Number: 88-51680
McPeak, Ron, Glantz, Dale, and Shaw, Carole
    The Amber Forest: Beauty and Biology of California's Submarine Forests

Printed in Singapore through Palace Press.

Table of Contents

Dedication

We dedicate this book to our spouses, Lynn Hisey Glantz, Mary McPeak and John Shaw, who gave us moral support and constructive criticism at appropriate times, and to our co-workers who volunteered their time to answer questions and review our work.

Ronald H. McPeak
Dale A. Glantz
Carole R. Shaw

Foreword

Preparing a foreword to *The Amber Forest* is somewhat akin to introducing George Washington to a town council meeting: anything I could possibly say would be dwarfed by the eminent quality of what follows. It is better to let the reader judge the excellence of this book for his or her self, rather than delay that pleasant experience by a foreword full of flowery praise. It might be informative, however, for me to describe the backgrounds of our authors. Why are they so highly qualified to produce a book about undersea life? Why did they choose to write about kelp, a seaweed that many people regard as slimy and unsightly when it lies rotting on the beach and a damn nuisance when it entangles them while wading or swimming at the seashore?

Ron McPeak and Dale Glantz are a new breed, ocean farmers, employed by Kelco Division of Merck & Co., Inc., in San Diego, to increase productivity of the crops it harvests, luxuriant canopies of the Amber Forest. These are individuals who have devoted their lives to enriching the sea and capturing its many wonders on film for us to marvel at. They have witnessed the captivating beauty of countless seascapes. Their bodies have experienced the churning violence and powerful forces that ruthlessly destroy entire marine communities when great storms sweep through the Amber Forest. Their toils have restored large tracts of Amber Forest torn out by waves, grazed to extinction by plagues of sea urchins, or lost to unwise practices of waste disposal. They are widely respected for their knowledge and understanding of undersea ecology and have contributed to the large body of scientific literature on kelp communities.

Carole Shaw is a sportdiver and underwater photographer who has glided among the fronds of the Amber Forest innumerable times. She brings to the team years of experience as a freelance writer, photographer, and editor.

The authors are deeply motivated to communicate to their fellow humans their glimpses of this exciting world that lies near the edge of the sea. Their book is a labor of love: love of the undersea and its wondrous denizens. They have culled the best from thousands of photographs and set out for us their story of a fascinating assemblage of marine creatures and the benefits we derive therefrom.

Dear Reader, I hope that your experience reading *The Amber Forest* will be as pleasurable as mine has been.

Wheeler J. North
Kerckhoff Marine Laboratory
California Institute of Technology

Introduction

Rising from the rocky nearshore substrate of the world's cool but temperate oceans is a giant, amber-colored seaweed known as *Macrocystis pyrifera*. Like Jack's magical beanstalk, *Macrocystis pyrifera* shoots skyward at a phenomenal rate until it finally reaches the surface. Once there, kept afloat by gas-filled bladders called pneumatocysts, it continues to grow horizontally at a rate of up to two feet per day. The spreading fronds form a golden-hued canopy that stands out against the vivid blue of the sea. Unusual? Yes. But equally beautiful and useful.

Macrocystis pyrifera is commonly called giant kelp. Originally, kelp referred to the potash-rich ash that was derived from burning marine plants. However, general usage of the term has evolved over the years to mean any of the large brown seaweeds.

Forests of kelp occur in both the Northern and Southern Hemispheres. Species of *Macrocystis* are common from Argentina, through the Straits of Magellan to Chile, off South Africa, Australia, New Zealand, and many sub-Antarctic islands. In the Northern Hemisphere, the forests occur from central Baja California, Mexico, to Sitka, Alaska. They are especially well developed off the coast of California from San Diego to Santa Cruz.

Plate 1.

A forest of giant kelp plants towers over a bright orange-gold garibaldi (*Hypsypops rubicundus*) and a cigar-shaped señorita (*Oxyjulis californica*). The garibaldi, which can grow to 14 inches in length, is one of the most colorful inhabitants of kelp forests from southern California to central Baja California, Mexico. A favorite of underwater photographers, the garibaldi does not shy away from divers who "invade" its territory. Perhaps this gutsy little fish senses it is a protected species in California waters.

The señorita provides a service to the garibaldi and a few of the other fishes that inhabit the forest. It sets up a "cleaning station" and picks parasites and bits of dying tissue from the patient fishes.

Plate 1

Kelp forests have attracted the attention of mankind for centuries. Giant kelp was eaten by primitive peoples. Populations of Chumash Indians who lived along the coast of California as long as 10,000 years ago concentrated their villages in the vicinity of these forests, probably because they recognized them as a source of fish and other edible creatures.

Early explorers learned to use kelp as an aid to navigation. Drifting kelp meant land was near. Attached kelp indicated the presence of rocks and dangerous shallows. Skippers who did not heed kelp's warning often found their ships run aground.

As early as the 1800s, forests of giant kelp were recognized for their ecological importance. Charles Darwin, during the 1834 visit of the *HMS Beagle* to Chile, noted that forests of giant kelp provided shelter, substrate, and food for millions of animals.

With the introduction of self-contained underwater breathing apparatus (scuba) more than a century later, a reasonable understanding of *Macrocystis* and its ecology began to emerge as researchers explored the underwater environment. In 1955, Conrad Limbaugh of the Scripps Institution of Oceanography in La Jolla, California, was the first to provide a detailed account of the kelp bed environment based on scuba diving experiences. Dr. Wheeler J. North, formerly of Scripps and now with the California Institute of Technology, soon followed with exhaustive studies of his own. As a result of the interest generated by the work of those two research pioneers, a large cadre of scientists has continued studying the many aspects of *Macrocystis* ecology.

Research has provided an understanding of the ecological importance of the forest and has led to the discovery of myriad uses for derivatives of kelp. The result has been the growth of a multi-million dollar kelp harvesting and processing industry in California.

Plate 2.
Each year during March or April, young fronds of *Macrocystis* plants off the Monterey Peninsula in California reach the surface, producing canopies. By July or August, the canopies in some areas become so dense that almost no sunlight reaches the ocean floor beneath them. Divers exploring the forest below these canopies — even during daylight hours in mid-summer — frequently need underwater lights to see more than a few feet.

Plate 2

In the pages that follow, we will share the beauty, complexity, and dynamics of forests of *Macrocystis pyrifera* that grow along the coast of California and Baja California. We will explain how the plants grow, change with age, reproduce, and die. We will discuss how people have used kelp over the centuries and why, as we approach the 21st century, the kelp forests are important as a source of food and as a submarine playground. In conclusion, we will discuss what is being done to preserve this unique and valuable resource we call **The Amber Forest**.

Plate 3.

"*If you see beds of weedes* (Macrocystis), *take heed of them and keep off from them.*" The wreck of a large sailing vessel off the coast of San Diego, California, in an area thick with kelp, is testimony that the above warning, recorded by Sebastian Cabote in the 16th century, is still valid today. Generally speaking, the presence of growing kelp plants signals to mariners the presence of potentially dangerous rocky reefs not far beneath the ocean surface.

Plate 3

Plates 4 - 6.

"The number of living creatures of all Orders, whose existence intimately depends on kelp is wonderful. A great volume might be written, describing the inhabitants of one of these beds of seaweed." In the 1800s Charles Darwin recognized the importance of *Macrocystis* as food, substrate, and shelter for myriad animals, just a few of which are shown here.

The Spanish shawl (*Flabellinopsis iodinea*), shown crawling on a giant kelp frond (Plate 4), is one of many species of shell-less snails called nudibranchs that inhabit forests of *Macrocystis*. This seemingly vulnerable animal, which grows to a length of two inches, seems to flaunt its presence in the face of potential predators. However, it is believed that the nudibranch's bright coloration actually serves as a warning that the creature is foul-tasting and should be avoided.

Tiny white specks, new colonies of the bryozoan *Membranipora membranacea*, develop on blades of *Macrocystis* (Plate 5). A grass rockfish (*Sebastes rastrelliger*), usually a bottom-dweller, takes refuge in the forest (Plate 6).

Plate 4

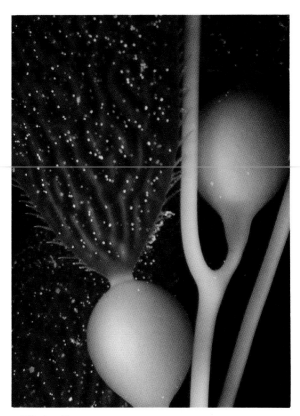

Plate 5

Plate 6

13

Part I

The Forest

Plate 7.
Macrocystis fronds shoot skyward toward the life-giving sun.

Plate 7

Chapter 1

Giant Kelp

Giant kelp, *Macrocystis pyrifera*, is appropriately named. One of twenty species of kelp found off the coast of California, this highly evolved marine alga is the largest marine plant known on earth. Under optimal growing conditions, individual plants can achieve a length of over 100 feet in little more than a year.

Dependent on sunlight for growth, giant kelp is generally found in shallow waters ranging in depth from 20 to 80 feet. Sunlight easily penetrates such depths, and the plants are spared the relentless pounding of the surf typical in more shallow areas. There are exceptions, however. In the extremely clear waters off California's Channel Islands and Punta Banda, Baja California, giant kelp has been known to grow from depths of 130 feet.

Each mature giant kelp plant consists of a holdfast, a cluster of reproductive blades called sporophylls, and anywhere from a few to several hundred fronds. It lacks a root system. It is the holdfast, a mass of intertwining, branching strands called haptera, that anchors each plant firmly to the rocky substrate.

Plates 8 - 10.
The depth range of giant kelp varies from site to site. In tide pools at San Quintin, Baja California, Mexico, *Macrocystis* spreads over intertidal rocks or floats in the shallow water (Plate 8) withstanding constant surge and crashing waves (Plate 10).

Elsewhere, such as off California's Channel Islands and at Punta Banda, in Mexico, where water is exceptionally clear, populations can grow from extreme depths (Plate 9).

Plate 8

Plate 9

Plate 10

All parts of the giant kelp plant possess the capacity for photosynthesis. Those above the holdfast also have the ability to take nutrients such as phosphates and nitrates from the water. However, it is the fronds that have reached the surface, forming a canopy exposed to large amounts of sunlight, that carry out these processes most effectively. Other parts of the giant kelp plant are largely dependent upon the transfer of energy from the canopy for growth.

The fronds, which grow from the apex of the holdfast, resemble vines. They are composed of long stipes (or stems), leaf-like blades with wrinkled surfaces, and gas-filled bladders that keep the fronds afloat and prevent them from falling to the ocean floor. Bladders come in many forms ranging from spheres to elongate, pear-shaped structures.

Giant kelp is extremely flexible. Firmly affixed to the substrate, it sways gently with the surge and bends gracefully in the direction of the currents when the sea is calm. Huge swells and crashing waves generated by storms, on the other hand, cause it to flail violently. Yet, except under unusually severe conditions, it survives.

Plates 11 - 13.

A mature giant kelp plant consists of a single holdfast, a cluster of reproductive blades called sporophylls, and anywhere from a few to several hundred fronds.

The holdfast, seen partially exposed beneath a large cluster of sporophylls (Plate 11) looks like the root system of land-based plants. However, while it attaches the plant to the substrate, the holdfast does not take nutrients from the soil as roots do.

Fronds (Plate 12), which grow from the apex of the holdfast, resemble twisted vines. Each, with its many attached blades and bladders, provides a place of refuge for fishes such as the school of blacksmith (*Chromis punctipennis*) seen here.

Gas-filled bladders at the base of each blade (Plate 13) float the plant in the water column.

18

Plate 11

Plate 12

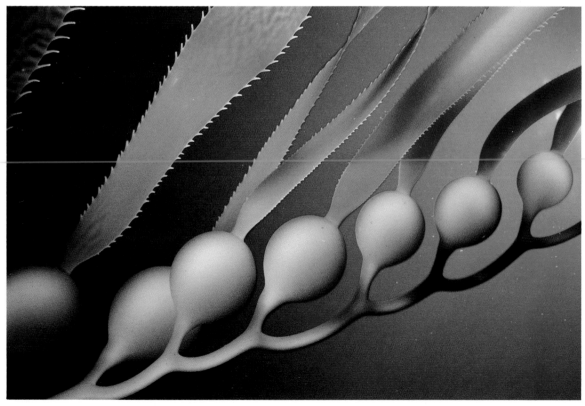

Plate 13

19

Plate 14.

All parts of *Macrocystis* possess the capacity for photosynthesis, the process by which plants convert water and carbon dioxide into carbohydrates, using sunlight as a source of energy, with the aid of chlorophyll. The blade, with its large surface area increased by wrinkling, accounts for most photosynthesis in giant kelp. Blades also have the ability to take nutrients such as phosphates and nitrates from the surrounding water. Nutrients taken up from the water and carbohydrates produced by photosynthesis are translocated to the growing regions of the plant by a system of conducting cells within the plant.

Plate 14

Chapter 2

Life Cycle and Growth

Giant kelp plants seen by visitors to the west coast of North America represent just one stage in the life cycle of the Amber Forest.

The cycle begins when sporophylls, specialized reproductive blades located at the base of mature plants, liberate spores into the surrounding water, much as a dandelion liberates wind-borne seeds into the air. The sporophylls of a single plant can produce trillions of microscopic spores annually. However, conditions must be just right if the spores are to develop into new plants.

When adequate light and room for attachment and growth are available among the mature plants of the forest, the tiny spores settle and develop into male and female gametophytes, which in turn produce sperm and eggs. Fertilization of the gametophyte egg results in an embryonic plant, a microscopic sporophyte. It is this sporophyte that, in time, will become an Amber Giant.

En route to becoming a mature plant, the sporophyte first develops into a single heart-shaped blade. As many as 1,000 blades can carpet an area measuring ten square

Plate 15.
The life cycle of giant kelp involves an alternation of generations between the "adult" sporophyte that produces spores and the microscopic gametophyte plant that produces sperm or eggs.

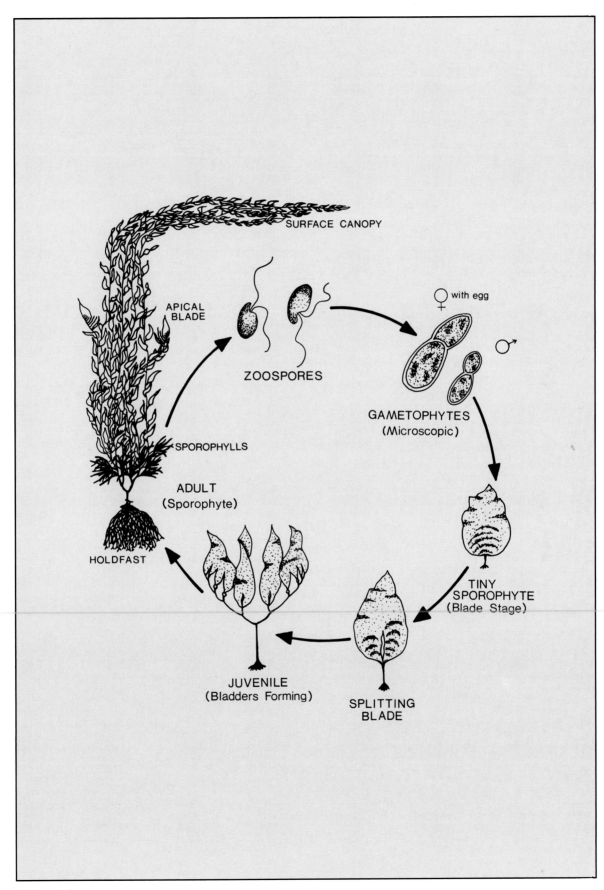

SURFACE CANOPY

APICAL BLADE

ZOOSPORES

♀ with egg

♂

GAMETOPHYTES
(Microscopic)

SPOROPHYLLS

ADULT
(Sporophyte)

HOLDFAST

TINY
SPOROPHYTE
(Blade Stage)

JUVENILE
(Bladders Forming)

SPLITTING
BLADE

Plate 15

23

feet. Within a few weeks, when the plant reaches three to four inches in height, it begins to split into two identical blades. Even before the new blades are completely formed, they also begin to split. Two become four. Four become eight, and so on.

Fronds develop as the young blades thicken at the base, produce bladders, and grow toward the surface. The apical blade, a specialized growth blade located at the tip of each frond, constantly produces new "regular" blades as it grows upward and eventually becomes part of the surface canopy.

When sunlight is ample, ocean temperatures are in the 50°F - 65°F range, and nutrients are plentiful, fronds that make up the canopy can grow at a rate of up to two feet per day. Juvenile fronds near the base of the plant might grow two inches per day, a phenomenal rate when considered as a percentage increase in size. Because the juvenile fronds receive little direct sunlight, they depend upon the transfer of energy from the canopy for growth. The process of transferring growth products from the canopy to other parts of the plant is known as translocation.

A giant kelp plant can live for up to six years, or perhaps longer. During that time, fronds that make up the plant continually develop, mature, and finally break away in a process called sloughing. New fronds push toward the surface to replace the sloughing fronds. Within a few months, they too will mature, die, and break away.

Meanwhile, sporophylls at the base of the plant continue to produce and release spores into the water. The life cycle continues.

Plate 16.

A female sheephead (*Semi-cossyphus pulcher*) swims near slender golden sporophylls, the reproductive blades of this kelp plant.

Plate 17.

When adequate light is available, the microscopic spores settle and develop into male and female gameto-phytes, shown here as seen through a microscope. Females produce a single egg. Males, of which several are visible across the top of the photo, are smaller and have more cells than the females. Males produce thousands of sperm.

Plate 18.

Inch-high blades, tiny sporophytes, compete with animals and other plants for space on the ocean floor.

Plate 16

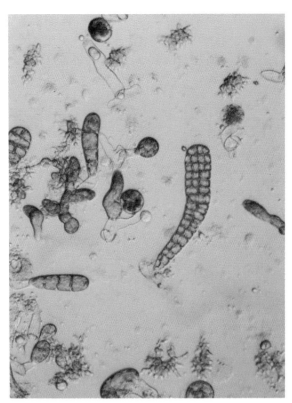

Plate 17

Plate 18

Plates 19 - 21.

Sporophytes of all kelp species start out as a blade that, when small, looks alike from species to species. As it grows, the blade stage of each species takes on characteristics particular to that species.

The blade stage of giant kelp, wrinkled and transparent, can be distinguished from those of other species when only a few inches high (Plate 19). This three-inch tall blade is just beginning to split at its base.

The base of a six-inch high blade (Plate 20) shows the beginnings of five splits. The first bladder is beginning to form and appears as a slight swelling at the bottom right of this plant. The base of this blade will thicken, elongate, produce bladders, and finally develop into fronds (Plate 21).

Plate 19

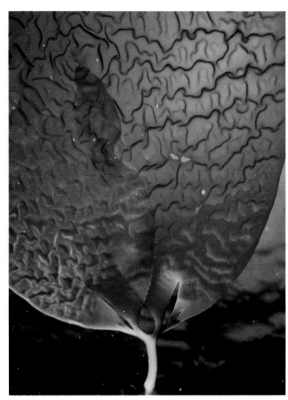

Plate 20

Plate 21

Plate 22.

Fronds of juvenile plants continue to grow toward the surface.

Plate 23.

The apical blade, located at the tip of the frond, produces new "regular" blades as it grows toward the surface. At about five months of age, the apical blade stops producing new blades.

Plate 24.

In time, the frond will begin to die and eventually slough away, as the light colored fronds seen here on this mature plant are doing.

Plate 22

Plate 23

Plate 24

Plate 25.

Sunlight filters through a thin canopy, creating a forest that has brightness and shadows. Young fronds that have reached the canopy can grow at a phenominal rate when sunlight is ample, nutrients such as nitrate and phosphate are plentiful in the water, and temperatures are cool. Researchers at Scripps Institution of Oceanography in La Jolla, California have measured fronds elongating at a rate of 24 inches per day.

Plate 25

Chapter 3

The Ever-Changing Forest

It is natural for forests of *Macrocystis pyrifera* to experience periods of dense growth followed by thinning or even complete disappearance. The cause of these changes can be as subtle as a rise of a few degrees in ocean temperature or the competition among growing plants for space and nourishment. Or it can be as obvious as frequent and ferocious storms.

The survival of individual kelp plants is far from assured. As they grow, plants must compete for light and nutrients and for substrate to accommodate their constantly expanding holdfasts. They compete not only with plants of their own species for these precious commodities, but also with their forest relatives — the nineteen other species of kelp found off the coast of California. The size and shape of *Macrocystis pyrifera* forests are in a constant state of flux as other kelps either gain a foothold or lose ground to *Macrocystis*. The boundary changes are often so subtle that the casual observer is unlikely to notice them, even over a period of several years. However, scientists who monitor the growth of

Plates 26 - 28.

Forests of giant kelp can persist for years or change rapidly. The forests are influenced by changes in oceanographic conditions, grazing animals, or competition from other species of algae. It is often simply a matter of chance and timing that determines who will win the competitive struggle between seaweeds. In central California, near Carmel, bull kelp (*Nereocystis luetkeana*) competes with giant kelp for space, light, and nutrients (Plate 26).

Elk kelp (*Pelagophycus porra*), buoyed in the water column by a single bladder the size of a volleyball, spreads its twelve blades, measuring nearly 30 feet long, in a gentle current. This annual kelp competes with giant kelp off southern California and Baja California, Mexico (Plate 27).

Species of algae, competing in shallow water with giant kelp, frequently resemble a spring bloom of wild flowers. They carpet the bottom and reveal their vibrant colors, as seen at Los Coronados Islands, Baja California, Mexico (Plate 28).

Plate 26

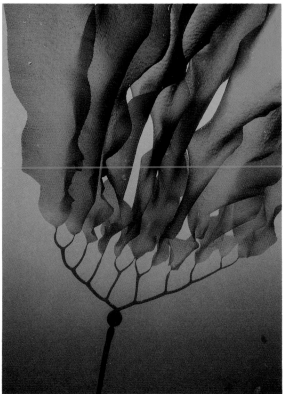

Plate 27

Plate 28

33

Macrocystis from the air and underwater are keenly aware of even minor shifts.

Once plants become established, they must be strong enough to withstand the whiplash effect of surge and lucky enough not to be over-grazed by the animals of the forest. Among the most voracious and prolific of the grazers is the sea urchin, a round, spine-covered animal that is especially fond of *Macrocystis*.

A young forest of *Macrocystis* is jungle-like, with plants so close together that swimming among them without becoming entangled would seem impossible for all but the smallest of creatures. From the surface, a mature forest appears equally dense. An underwater vantage point, however, reveals that such a forest is really made up of relatively few, widely scattered survivors whose lush canopies converge to cover a large area. As these adult plants grow old, they become less able to tolerate the forces of nature. One by one, they are weeded out.

The weeding-out process produces a forest whose canopy becomes increasingly sparse, allowing large amounts of sunshine to reach spores that have settled to the substrate. Eventually, if nutrients are also sufficient, the sunlight triggers a burst of new growth. Within a few months, a jungle of young plants emerges.

That is the normal course when weather conditions are benign.

When conditions are hostile, an entire forest can disappear almost overnight, and re-growth can be slow.

Storms that generate huge waves play havoc with the kelp forest. Underwater, such storms create a scene that resembles a topside hurricane. Usually-resilient plants are buffeted, twisted, and tangled until they are either broken or uprooted. As they are cast toward shore, the storm-tossed plants ensnare and finally uproot additional plants. Following a severe storm, it is not unusual to see

Plate 29.

A kelp bass (*Paralabrax clathratus*) glides through a young forest of giant kelp. The plants in this forest, only eight months old, are packed close together, several per square yard. Divers trying to swim through such a forest often become frustrated as fronds become entangled around their fins and other dive gear.

Each plant, secured by a holdfast that measures about six inches in diameter, has from four to six fronds. The first few fronds produced by a juvenile plant are thin and spindly and will probably never reach the surface to become part of the canopy.

As the forest ages, plants will be thinned out by the forces of nature. In such a forest there is often only one giant kelp plant for every 200 or more square feet of bottom.

34

Plate 29

beached kelp in mounds that stand more than ten feet high and contain thousands of individual plants.

Forests of *Macrocystis* are usually bathed by cool, nutrient-rich waters. Occasionally, however, an oceanic/ atmospheric phenomenon known as El Niño produces a warming trend that makes its way from the tropics to the coast of North America. If El Niño is potent, the kelp forests are certain to suffer.

The most severe El Niño on record reached North America in the fall of 1982, peaked in 1983, and lingered into 1984. This El Niño, which spread to Antarctica as well as across the Pacific to Japan, has been blamed for worldwide climatic deviations: destructive storms and flooding in usually arid regions, droughts elsewhere.

In the eastern Pacific Ocean, water temperatures climbed to almost ten degrees Fahrenheit above normal during El Niño. Highs in central California reached the mid-60s. In southern California, a high of 77.5°F was recorded.

The warming trend delighted swimmers, surfers, and scuba divers. But as the nutrient-rich, cool waters were replaced by nutrient-poor, warmer waters, kelp plants began to weaken. Temperature stress, nitrogen starvation, and reduced photosynthesis meant lowered growth rates and canopy loss. Poorly growing plants were especially susceptible to the destructive forces of violent storms spawned by El Niño. Once-luxuriant forests were thinned to just a few plants or disappeared completely.

Plants that survived El Niño produced enough spores to spark a rebirth of the forests by late 1984, when conditions again became favorable for growth. However, well into 1988, forests in some areas still had not returned to their pre-El Niño luxuriance.

Plates 30 - 32.
When conditions are hostile, as during a storm, an entire kelp forest can disappear overnight.

An uprooted plant (Plate 30) with bleached haptera slowly drifts through a forest of giant kelp off San Clemente Island, California. The plant, uprooted several weeks before the photograph was taken, lost the rich colors characteristic of growing haptera.

Plants that are not uprooted are often so severely thrashed during storms that they do not survive. The storm-damaged plant in Plate 31 has produced several new fronds. Because these small fronds will probably be unable to translocate sufficient material to support the large holdfast of this older plant, the holdfast will undoubtedly weaken and lose its grasp on the substrate.

Beach litter that results when kelp washes ashore varies from a few fronds to hundreds of tons of fronds. At La Jolla Shores, in San Diego, California, the beach is nearly obliterated by kelp that washed ashore during a severe storm (Plate 32).

Plate 30

Plate 31

Plate 32

Plate 33.

Occasionally, an oceanic/atmospheric phenomenon known as El Niño produces a warming trend that makes its way from the tropics to California and Baja California, Mexico, causing destruction of the kelp beds.

During El Niño conditions, giant kelp struggles to grow in the nutrient-poor warm water. Ragged and tatered fronds, photographed at San Miguel Island, California, in September 1983 never reached the surface to produce canopies during the El Niño.

Plate 33

Plates 34 - 35.

Many interesting animals with tropical affinities are displaced hundreds of miles north of their normal range during the warming El Niño.

When pelagic red crabs, *Pleuroncodes planipes* (Plate 34), appear off the coast of California, it usually means El Niño conditions are present. These three-inch-long crabs sometimes drift ashore by the millions, littering California beaches.

The spiny boxfish, *Ostracion diaphanum* (Plate 35), normally occurs in the tropical Pacific from the Gulf of California to the Galapágos Islands. This four-inch specimen was photographed during the 1982-1984 El Niño, at Los Coronados Islands, Baja California, Mexico, several hundred miles north of its normal range.

Plate 34

Plate 35

Part II

The Forest as a Habitat

Plate 36.
A school of jack mackerel (*Trachurus symmetricus*) flashes through a forest of giant kelp at Anacapa Island, California.

Plate 36

Chapter 4

An Overview

Forests of giant kelp that grow along the west coast of North America from central California to central Baja California, Mexico, support an ecosystem in which nearly 800 species of animals have been identified. Studies have shown that a column of water in which a giant kelp plant grows can support several thousand times as many animals as a column of water stretching above a barren, sand-covered ocean floor.

Anyone who has ever dived among the lush vegetation of the kelp beds or gazed through the observation ports of a glassbottom boat skirting the fringes of one of these aquatic wonderlands can attest to the variety of life there.

Creatures found among the amber giants range in size from microscopic to gigantic. They include birds, mammals, invertebrates and, of course, fishes. Some, such as the huge, migratory gray whale, are transients that only rarely pass through the forest. Others, including several species of snails, live upon, hide among, or feed on the kelp plants or on bits of drifting kelp tissue.

Plates 37 - 38.
Animals found in the Amber Forest range from microscopic to gigantic. The bryozoan *Lichenopora buskiana* (Plate 37) is among the many species of tiny animals that settle upon giant kelp. *Lichenopora*, which settles in the wrinkles of giant kelp blades, filter-feeds on plankton that drifts through the forest.

The gray whale (*Eschrichtius robustus*), weighing many tons, often passes through the forests during its annual migration from the breeding lagoons of Baja California, Mexico, to the Bering Sea. This whale (Plate 38) wallowed lazily in the kelp for several days before continuing northward.

Plate 37

Plate 38

The forest population changes gradually from location to location as one travels southward along the coast. There is considerable overlapping of species from one area to another, especially where fishes are concerned. It is not unusual for underwater explorers who dive the kelp beds in Carmel Bay, off central California, to see black rockfish, kelp greenlings, and wolf eels, whose range extends to the frigid waters of Alaska, co-existing with kelp rockfish, olive rockfish and kelp surfperch, fishes commonly found in southern California waters. Other fishes usually associated with southern California — garibaldi, sheephead, and kelp bass, for example — are a common sight in kelp beds hundreds of miles south of the U.S.-Mexican border, where tropical species such as the porcupinefish, triggerfish, and butterflyfish are seen.

Scientists who study the forest ecosystem generally divide the kelp habitat into three areas or neighborhoods: the holdfast, midwater fronds, and surface canopy. Animals that can crawl or swim frequently migrate from one area to another. Sessile animals such as hydroids and bryozoans settle for life in any of the three. Some animals leave the forest completely when the frond they call home either sloughs off from the canopy or when the entire plant of which the frond is a part is torn from the substrate, as by a storm. When this happens, the resultant drifting or beached kelp is transformed into a fourth, usually short-lived neighborhood.

Beached kelp, or kelp wrack, is generally considered a nuisance because it attracts hordes of pesky flies and, in time, decays, filling the sea air with a foul odor. Drifting kelp, on the other hand, is sought out by anglers, who know that large, tasty fishes often gather beneath the tangled fronds. The prized catches are albacore (*Thunnus alalunga*), yellowtail (*Seriola dorsalis*), and dolphinfish (*Coryphaena hippurus*). These predators feed upon smaller fishes that seek protection near the transient kelp.

Plates 39 - 41.
Many species of invertebrates live upon, hide among, or feed on kelp plants. Some are obvious; others are seen only by the careful observer.

The proliferating sea anemone (*Epiactis prolifera*) is a common inhabitant of the holdfast and basal portions of giant kelp (Plate 39). Members of this species come in a variety of colors – from soft orange to pink, red, or vivid maroon.

The seastar *Pisaster giganteus* (Plate 40) which develops from a small planktonic larvae, may spend its early days on *Macrocystis* fronds. Eventually, it makes its way to the rocky substrate below, where it develops into a large animal with an arm span of more than two feet.

The red rock shrimp (*Lysmata californica*) is one of several species of shrimps that live in the kelp forest (Plate 41). It is often referred to as the "cleaner" shrimp because it picks parasites, dead tissue, and almost anything else removable from other animals, including the garibaldi (*Hypsypops rubicundus*) and the California spiny lobster (*Panulirus interruptus*).

Plate 39

Plate 40

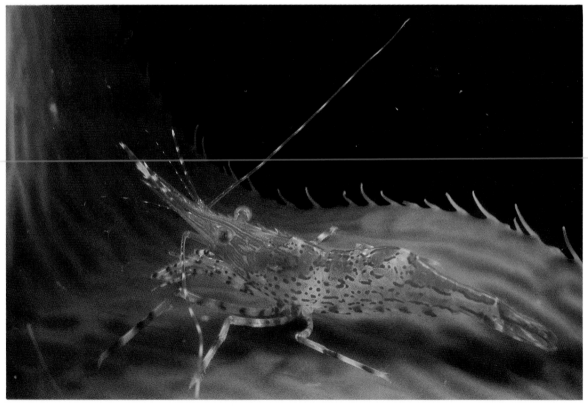

Plate 41

Without a doubt, the amber giants are vital to the survival of a complex underwater ecosystem. The uniqueness of that ecosystem can best be illustrated through observations of some of the hundreds of creatures that congregate in the forest.

Plates 42 - 43.

Forest populations change gradually as one travels southward along the Pacific Coast. The wolf eel, *Anarrhichthys ocellatus* (Plate 42), commonly seen in kelp forests off central California, does not occur off Baja California, Mexico. Although it appears dangerous, the wolf eel, seen here peering from a sponge-covered reef speckled with *Corynactis californica* sea anemones, is actually quite docile and is frequently handled by experienced divers.

The moray eel, *Gymnothorax mordax* (Plate 43), is often observed in forests off southern California and throughout Baja California, Mexico. This moray is surrounded by red rock shrimp (*Lysmata californica*).

Plate 42

Plate 43

Plate 44.

Rockfishes (*Sebastes* spp) are common in kelp forests of central and southern California. Some species, such as the gopher rockfish, *Sebastes carnatus*, occur as solitary individuals on the rocky reefs that support giant kelp. Others form dense schools beneath the canopy or among the fronds.

Plate 45.

The balloon- or porcupine-fish, *Diodon holocanthus*, is one of many tropical species found in the kelp forests of central Baja California, Mexico. When disturbed, this slow-moving creature defends itself by inflating with water or air and erecting its long, sharp spines. In addition, the skin of this fish contains a weak toxin that wards off potential predators.

Plate 44

Plate 45

Plates 46 - 47.

Kelp set adrift by storms can float at sea for many months. This drift patch or kelp paddy (Plate 46), seemingly uninhabited now, might become a resting place for birds or a temporary home for many species of juvenile fishes. Two-inch-long treefish, *Sebastes serriceps* (Plate 47), seek refuge among a kelp paddy's twisted fronds. They will settle on the ocean floor in shallow water when the paddy nears shore. Adult treefish are frequently seen resting among rocky reefs where forests of giant kelp occur.

Plate 46

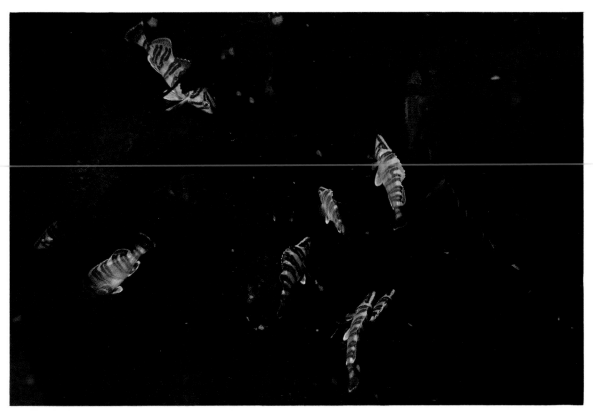

Plate 47

Chapter 5

The Holdfast

The holdfast of each giant kelp plant serves a dual purpose in the ecology of the forest. As its name implies, the holdfast holds the kelp plant fast to the substrate and keeps it from being torn away by the constant shock of surge and wave action. But at the same time, the maze formed by the intertwining, root-like strands of haptera that make up the holdfast provides a home for more than 175 species of marine creatures.

The holdfast of a young plant is made up of brightly colored haptera: blue, purple, pink or red. On plants that are several years old, the brightly colored, new haptera grow over an inner core of dead haptera that have turned dark brown.

Many creatures that seldom see the light of day live in the inner, dead portion of holdfasts. One of them is the kelp gribble (*Phycolimnoria algarum*), a small, whitish pill bug-like crustacean that chews its way through the haptera, making a series of tunnels as it goes. Tiny holes, respiratory openings that pierce the surface of the haptera, are the only signs that this creature works within.

Plate 48.
The holdfast of a three-year-old plant, about two feet in diameter and two feet high, will continue to increase in size as the plant ages. Young haptera, root-like in appearance, grow over old haptera, eventually producing a cone-shaped structure.

Plate 48

Sea anemones, which look more like flowers than the animals they really are, along with colorful sponges and other sessile creatures, use the sturdy strands of haptera as substrate for attachment. Low, squat proliferating anemones (*Epiactis prolifera*) are common, often with many juveniles attached around the base of the adult animal. The tentacles of the proliferating anemones are armed with a potent arsenal – stinging cells or nemato-cysts, which serve a dual purpose. They protect the anemones from predators and assist them in capturing food.

Skinny-armed brittle stars grasp the haptera with two or more of their five arms, while their remaining arms gather food in the form of plankton from the surrounding water. These unusual looking relatives of the sea star or "starfish" family are sometimes present in such great numbers that their projecting arms give the holdfast a hairy appearance.

A much larger animal, the swell shark (*Cephalo-scyllium ventriosum*), secures its purse-shaped egg case to the haptera by means of entangling tendrils. The devel-oping shark embryo appears as a silhouette when sun-light penetrates the translucent egg case.

Juvenile abalone and shrimp are among the creatures that turn to the holdfast as a place of refuge from preda-tors. These small creatures spend most of their time tucked away among the crevices formed by the branch-ing haptera, venturing out only occasionally to feed. When they do emerge to feed, these animals often become food themselves for predators. The kelp rockfish (*Sebastes atrovirens*), aided by its large, keen-sighted eyes and huge mouth, is one predator that can easily detect and devour tiny shrimp and other shrimp-like animals that sometimes emerge from a holdfast by the thousands.

In addition to the animals of the forest that depend

Plate 49.
Haptera on a young plant begin as small, colorful pro-tuberances that continue to elongate and eventually branch. Branching continues until the haptera reach the bottom and firmly attach. Once the haptera attach, they change color, turning yellow or brown. Lacy white bryozo-ans (*Membranipora mem-branacea*) have attached to the old haptera of this plant.

Plates 50 - 51.
Researchers at the Scripps Institution of Oceanography have identified more than 175 species of animals living on and in the holdfasts of giant kelp. A small kelpfish (Plate 50), rests on the holdfast of giant kelp while brittle stars, *Ophiothrix spiculata*, with only the tips of their arms exposed, seek refuge among the branch-ing haptera.

A seastar, *Linckia columbi-ana* (Plate 51) crawls over the holdfast of a young plant.

Plate 49

Plate 50

Plate 51

upon the holdfast for food and substrate, there are transients that merely pass through the holdfast community on their journey to the upper regions of the forest — regions equally rich and diverse in inhabitants as the holdfast.

Plates 52 - 53.

The swell shark, *Cephaloscyllium ventriosum* (Plate 52), occurs among rocky reefs and on sand within kelp forests of southern California and Baja California, Mexico. Members of this species are especially common near Santa Barbara, California, where dozens of them can be seen clustered near the bases of *Macrocystis*. The docile swell shark is so-named because it swells when disturbed. The animal shown here is approximately three feet long.

After mating, the female swell shark lays leathery, purse-shaped egg cases, each bearing a single egg. Plate 53, photographed near Santa Barbara, shows the yolk mass developing within the case and tendrils attaching the case to the haptera.

Plate 52

Plate 53

Plate 54.

The kelp rockfish (*Sebastes atrovirens*), seen here hovering among giant kelp blades, are active predators of many of the thousands of tiny animals who venture from the security of the holdfast at night. Some kelp forests harbor hundreds of these rockfish, which hang motionless in the water column waiting for dusk to arrive and feeding time to begin.

Plate 54

Chapter 6

The Midwater Fronds

Each frond of a giant kelp plant resembles a high-rise apartment building or hotel that serves a variety of residents and visitors who are intent upon going about the business of living their lives. The looks, names, and actions of the critters that frequent the kelp bed high-rise might seem strange to their human counterparts, but that is what makes the animals so fascinating.

Tremendous communities of tiny filter feeders often completely cover the stem-like stipes, gas-filled bladders, and leafy blades of the fronds. These animals, which include disc-shaped bryozoans and feathery hydroids, continuously sweep the water with specialized appendages, filtering out the plankton and organic detritus that drift through the forest. Where hydroids are numerous, the kelp appears to be covered with a very fine fuzz.

The maximum lifespan of a *Macrocystis* frond is approximately six months. Encrusting bryozoans, such as *Membranipora membranacea*, which prefers giant kelp as a substrate, have evolved a rapid life cycle that

Plates 55 - 57.

Fronds of giant kelp are home for myriad animals that seek food, shelter, or substrate upon which to attach. Among them: the colorful blue and yellow *Mexichromis porterae* nudibranch (Plate 55), shown crawling over the apical region of a young kelp frond; the purple-ringed top snail, *Calliostoma annulatum* (Plate 56), which is especially abundant in central California; and kelp scallops, *Leptopecten monotimeris* (Plate 57).

The half dollar-sized kelp scallops occasionally settle on giant kelp by the thousands. They became so abundant on young *Macrocystis* off Point Loma in San Diego, California, in 1977 that the affected plants actually sank under the weight of the molluscs. Nearly 2,000 scallops were collected from a single plant that had collapsed to the ocean floor.

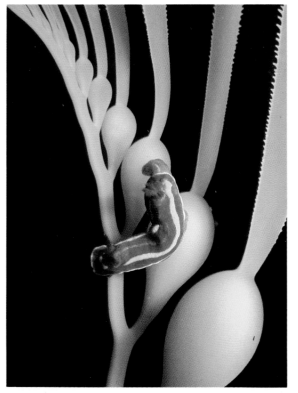

Plate 55

Plate 56

Plate 57

matches that of their host plant. The bryozoans settle on the kelp as microscopic triangular larvae that soon become visible as tiny white specks. Within a few days of settling, the bryozoans are capable of reproduction. In little more than three weeks, the individual "specks" that make up the bryozoan colony enlarge, coalesce, and form a layer of lacy white crust.

The sessile bryozoans and many other tiny animals that live on giant kelp are easy prey for nudibranchs, the ocean's carnivorous answer to the ordinary garden slug. Two nearly identical species of nudibranchs, the frost spot (*Corambe pacifica*) and Steinberg's dorid (*Doridella steinbergae*), live perfectly camouflaged among the white, encrusting bryozoans. The reticular pattern on the backs of these flattened, shell-less molluscs mimicks the lacy appearance of the bryozoan colonies. Damaged bryozoan colonies and the narrow, tightly coiled bands of eggs laid by the nudibranchs betray to human observers the presence of these voracious predators.

The bright coloration of other soft-bodied nudibranchs, such as the vibrant purple and orange *Flabellinopsis iodinea*, or Spanish shawl, makes them stand out against the kelp. But at the same time, conspicuous coloration warns other animals that the nudibranch is not a tasty meal.

The California black sea hare (*Aplysia vaccaria*) is a large, leathery, plain looking relative of the nudibranch that can grow up to 24 inches in length and weigh up to 20 pounds. Vegetarians, members of this species sometimes venture up the fronds when ocean conditions are calm in order to graze on blades of kelp. Their dark bodies, which range in color from reddish brown to black, look out of place clinging precariously to the slender fronds. Sudden surges of water can abruptly dislodge the animals and send them plopping unceremoniously back to the ocean floor.

Plate 58.
Small tree-like hydroids, with potent stinging capsules throughout their tissues for protection and capturing prey, join the developing bryozoans on a *Macrocystis* blade and bladder. A triangle-shaped flatworm (barely visible just below and to the left of the hydroids) glides toward the bryozoans. To the left of the hydroids is a small dove snail (*Mitrella carinata*).

Plate 59.
A giant kelpfish (*Heterostichus rostratus*) hides among bryozoan-covered fronds, as it waits for prey. This species can grow to two feet long and can change colors to match surrounding algae.

Plate 58

Plate 59

Several species of shelled molluscs crawl over the fronds of the midwater region. Notable among them are the purple-ringed top snail (*Calliostoma annulatum*) and the blue top snail (*Calliostoma ligatum*), which move about the forest munching on the kelp as well as bryozoans, hydroids, and organic detritus. These snail species sparkle like ornaments on a Christmas tree as the sun's rays reflect from their brilliantly colored shells.

Also common in the forests is the brown-shelled Norris's top snail (*Norrisia norrisi*), which feeds mainly on brown algae such as *Macrocystis*. This top snail clings to the stipe with its bright orange foot for balance. Then, using its radula, a ribbon-like structure armed with minute teeth, it scrapes the surface of the kelp and draws bits of plant tissue into its mouth. This method of feeding leaves barely visible tracks on the surface of the plant.

Small crustaceans with unusual names like amphipods, isopods, and mysids are the "insects" of the forest. In large numbers they swim and crawl among the foliage. Many of them are transparent and are thus nearly invisible to all but the most keen-sighted of visitors to the kelp community. All provide food for fishes and other animals.

The inch-long kelp-curler amphipod, *Ampithoe humeralis*, has evolved a unique method for protecting itself and its young from predators. This shrimp-like critter fashions a cigar-shaped chamber by deftly folding a kelp blade and securing the edges with a sticky, glue-like substance. At each end of the chamber, the kelp-curler leaves a small opening through which it can come and go.

The fishes of the forest are of two kinds: those that are transients, passing through the forest in search of food, and those that are residents, making the forest their permanent home.

Plates 60 - 61.

The kelp-curler amphipod (*Ampithoe humeralis*), which relies on kelp for food and shelter, has developed a unique method for protecting itself and its young from predators. The inch-long amphipod folds a *Macrocystis* blade and glues the edges to form a small chamber in which to take refuge (Plate 60). In Plate 61, an adult kelp-curler and two juveniles peer from a chamber that has been pulled apart by researchers to allow observation of these secretive animals.

When scattered throughout the forest in small numbers, kelp-curlers usually cause no damage to their host plants. However, in 1985, these amphipods were present in such large numbers in kelp beds off Point Loma in San Diego, California, that the animals' grazing caused their host plants to die.

Plate 60

Plate 61

Anchovies, yellowtail, mackerel, and barracuda are among the transients. The anchovies (*Engraulis mordax*) maneuver around the columns of kelp in tight schools, flashing and sparkling as their silver bodies and moving gill plates reflect rays of sunshine. Sometimes they cruise about almost casually. At other times they react nervously to every movement in the water. Predators lurk.

The resident kelp bass (*Paralabrax clathratus*), whose shape and camouflaging coloration enable it to "disappear" into the foliage, lies in wait. This predator as well as the many large, fast-moving transient fishes might strike the school. Following a strike, the surviving anchovies quickly leave. All that remains of the school are hundreds of scales drifting slowly down through the water column like so many silver snowflakes.

California sheephead (*Semicossyphus pulcher*), a species of wrasse that can weigh over 40 pounds, are territorial fish that patrol the kelp forest and rocky reefs by day. They are one of a few species of kelp forest fishes that change sex during their lifetime. Sheephead begin life as bright reddish orange juveniles with black spots on their fins. Their color gradually changes to light pink as they develop into females. Most, but not all, later change into males, which are usually bluish black with a red band around the central portion of the body. A mature male can be identified by the large fleshy hump on top of its head. This hump grows as the fish ages.

As night falls and the sheephead retire to the security of caves and crevices, the large, circular torpedo ray (*Torpedo californica*) emerges from its place on the forest floor. Members of this species, which can grow to three feet in diameter, resemble flying saucers as they hover in midwater. Also known as Pacific electric rays, they are capable of producing a shock of up to 80 volts with which they stun their prey. The electric ray's shock

Plate 62.
Dense schools of anchovies (*Engraulis mordax*), flash through the forest, maneuvering among the fronds while trying to elude predators such as kelp bass, rockfishes, or other large fishes that might be hiding nearby.

Plate 63.
A green-eyed kelp bass (*Paralabrax clathratus*), uses its large pectoral fins to balance in the water column. This species can grow to two feet in length and reach a maximum weight of 14 pounds.

Plate 62

Plate 63

is a threat to all creatures that come into contact with it, including people.

Among the creatures that are the most enjoyable to watch as they go about life in the kelp forest are the pinnipeds, including the sleek California sea lion and its chubby, basset hound-like cousin the harbor seal. The pinnipeds forage for food in kelp beds that grow near their rocky rookeries. Although they can weigh several hundred pounds each, the pinnipeds are by no means the largest visitors to the kelp forest. That honor goes to their fellow air-breathing marine mammal, the gray whale.

The gray whale (*Eschrichtius robustus*) sometimes visits the kelp forests during the annual 6,000-mile migration between its summer feeding grounds in the Bering Sea and its winter calving grounds off Baja California, Mexico. It is not clear exactly why the leviathans swim through the kelp. One theory is that the kelp forests provide a place where young calves, just weeks or months old, can hide from killer whales during the northward migration. It is believed that the kelp's gas-filled pneumatocysts, by reflecting sonar signals, interfere with the killer whale's ability to echolocate its young prey.

Another theory is that the gray whales feed in the forests. Although it is believed that they do not eat during the southerly migration, the gray whales do, while heading north, sometimes pause to snack on crustaceans that live among the kelp. Toothless, the grays use brush-like baleen that lines their huge mouths to strain the animals from the water and fronds. Rising from the mid-water region, fronds frequently draped from their mouths, the gray whales poke their snouts up through the canopy for a breath of sea air, dwarfing the birds and other animals that live on and in the uppermost region of the forest.

Plates 64 - 65.

The California sheephead (*Semicossyphus pulcher*) is common in forests of giant kelp that grow along the coast of southern California and Baja California, Mexico. Juveniles and adult males and females of this species of wrasse look quite different from each other.

Bright reddish-orange juvenile sheephead with black-spotted fins appear in nearshore waters as early as May each year. The juvenile shown in Plate 64 is approximately two inches long. It has its mouth agape in a fighting stance while sparring with another juvenile that is outside the picture area. Moments before this photo was taken, both fish were face-to-face, lip-to-lip, creating a "mirror-image."

All juvenile sheephead eventually develop into females, which are pink in color (Plate 65).

70

Plate 64

Plate 65

Plate 66.

Some, but not all, female sheephead transform into males when they are seven or eight years old. Males are usually brightly colored: black with a brilliant red or pink band in the center of the body and a white chin. Mature males develop a large, fleshy hump on top of the head. This hump becomes larger with age. These fish can weigh over forty pounds and live more than fifty years.

Plate 67.

The Pacific electric ray (*Torpedo californica*) emerges from its place on patches of soft bottom within the forest. The ray hovers in mid-water and feeds by shocking its prey with more than 80 volts of electricity. The electricity is created in specialized muscle cells located in the ray's back. Occasionally, an unsuspecting diver is jolted by the Pacific electric ray, learning quickly and painfully the value of staying clear of this well-armed creature.

73

Plate 66

Plate 67

Plates 68 - 69.

Marine mammals of varying sizes visit forests of giant kelp. Populations of pinnipeds (seals and sea lions), which are rapidly increasing along the west coast of California and Mexico, are frequently encountered in the kelp.

The California sea lion, *Zalophus californianus* (Plate 68), forages for food in forests of giant kelp. Sea lions are very fast swimmers. Many divers have been startled when the large pinnipeds swim directly at them, turning away just when a collision seems imminent.

The harbor seal, *Phoca vitulus* (Plate 69), also forages for food in kelp forests. The playful animal shown here swam up to the photographer and put its lips over the lens of the camera. Fortunately, the photograph was taken with a clean lens before this encounter.

Plate 68

Plate 69

Plates 70 - 71.

Gray whales (*Eschrichtius robustus*) sometimes pass through beds of *Macrocystis* on their annual migration between the breeding lagoons of Baja and the Bering Sea. These whales grow to 40 feet in length and weigh up to 35 tons (Plate 70).

Gray whales, which have no teeth, typically feed by filtering animals from the soft ocean floor using long brushlike baleen that hang from the roof of the mouth. A closeup of a gray whale with *Macrocystis* in its mouth (Plate 71) lends credence to some researchers' belief that the whale also feeds by straining small crustaceans from kelp foliage.

Plate 70

Plate 71

Chapter 7

The Surface Canopy

At the interface of sea and sky, golden canopies of giant kelp undulate endlessly to the rhythm of ocean swells. When canopies are lush, life abounds both above and below the intertwining fronds.

A well-developed canopy forms a buoyant mat on which birds can rest or perch as they search for prey. It also makes an excellent hiding place for small fishes, kelp crabs, snails, and other marine creatures. In areas where otters live, the fronds of the canopy double as anchors. When draped over an otter pup, a kelp frond holds the animal in place while the mother otter dives to the ocean floor to forage for food. In the same way, canopy fronds keep sleeping otters from drifting out to sea or into the surf line.

As in the other areas of the Amber Forest, life in the canopy resembles a game of hide-and-seek. Predators constantly hunt for their next meal. The hunted constantly try to avoid detection.

Keen-eyed birds recognize the kelp canopy as an excellent place to search for food.

Plates 72 - 73.
Dense canopies of giant kelp form on the surface when conditions for growth are good. Canopies in the foreground of Plate 72, taken from an airplane, in central California during the summer, are so dense that little light penetrates below.

Thick amber-colored canopies, photographed from a boat near La Jolla, California (Plate 73), reflect the sun. These canopies, which are too dense for a boat to pass through, provide safe lodging for many creatures.

Plate 72

Plate 73

Some species of sea gulls are fond of the abundant Norris's top snail, in spite of the fact that getting to the animal that lives within the shiny brown, protective shell is no easy task. Not to be denied its escargot treat, the bird has devised an ingenious method of defeating Mother Nature's game plan. It is a method that has been observed often at San Nicolas Island, the outermost of California's Channel Islands, where kelp, gulls, and Norris's top snails are all plentiful.

After picking a Norris's top snail off the canopy, the gull flies high above a rock outcropping and drops the snail onto the hard surface below. The snail, its shell broken by the crash landing, is then quickly consumed by the ever-hungry bird. Shell-strewn rock outcroppings around the perimeter of San Nicolas Island testify to the gull's appetite as well as its resourcefulness.

Members of the heron family — the great egret, snowy egret, and great blue heron — frequently stand on the edge of the canopy, necks stretched out over the water, patiently stalking fishes that live below. When the time is right, the heron uses its dagger-shaped bill to snatch its prey from the water. The tern, on the other hand, hovers above the canopy until it spots its prey. An elegant bird that can be identified in flight by its forked tail, black cap, and deep yellow bill, the tern captures its dinner by plunging head first into the water, making human observers reel with thoughts of the headache this manner of fishing must cause.

Among the preferred delicacies of the sea birds are the kelp clingfish (*Rimicola muscarum*) and kelp gunnel (*Ulvicola sanctaerosae*), which spend most of their lives in the canopy. Other favorites include several species of juvenile rockfishes, which remain in the canopy until they are large enough to fend for themselves at greater depths. The kelp clingfish grows to about two inches in length, while the kelp gunnel is about the length and

Plate 74.
The southern kelp crab (*Taliepus nuttalli*) is shown making its way to the canopy. The bright orange coloration of this animal indicates that it might have shed its protective shell not long before this photo was taken. This species of crab, like the common kelp crab (*Pugettia producta*), feeds on kelp and a variety of invertebrates. The crabs, in turn, become food for predators, including the California moray eel.

Plate 74

diameter of a pencil. Kelp-colored, these two species blend into the canopy. In addition, the kelp clingfish often escapes detection by clinging to the fronds by means of suction, using its specially adapted pelvic fins.

The sea otter (*Enhydra lutris*) dives among the kelp day and night trying to satisfy its voracious appetite. Because it has no blubber to protect it from the cool waters of the Pacific, the otter must eat about one fourth its body weight daily. That equates to as much as 15 pounds of sea creatures per otter per day: snails and kelp crabs that live in the canopy as well as abalone, sea urchins, clams, and crabs that live on or near the forest floor.

After a successful dive, the otter is frequently seen lying on its back in the canopy, working to open a hard-shelled animal with a rock or munching on a tasty morsel. The ingenious otter is one of only a few animal species that use tools.

Before commercial exploitation for its fur in the seventeenth and eighteenth centuries, the sea otter lived from northern Japan, along the Kamchatka coastline, across the Aleutian Islands, and southward along the west coast of North America. Today, sea otters are found from the Aleutian Islands to southern Alaska, in central California from Año Nuevo to Pismo Beach, and off southern California at San Nicolas Island. The population at San Nicolas Island, introduced in 1987 as part of a U. S. Fish and Wildlife Service translocation project, is the subject of a continuing controversy.

For the past decade, conservationists have argued that the sea otter population in California is in danger because it is restricted to a very small portion of its previous range. They argue that a single large oil spill could decimate the entire California sea otter population. Commercial fishermen and commercial divers, as well as many from the sportdiving community, argue that sea otters reintroduced to San Nicolas Island will soon

Plates 75 - 77.
Norris's top snail (*Norrisia norrisi*) is abundant on most brown seaweeds, including giant kelp. Young specimens (Plate 75) have a bright orange shell that matches the colorful "foot" used for locomotion. The shell of older specimens, which grow to almost three inches in diameter, is less colorful.

At San Nicolas Island, California, Western gulls (*Larus occidentalis*), Plate 76, have been observed feeding on the hard-shelled Norris's top snails. The gulls snatch the snails from the kelp canopy and then, flying above rocky outcroppings on shore, drop the molluscs, thus breaking their shells. Broken shells (Plate 77) are a sure sign that the gulls are eating well.

Plate 75

Plate 76

Plate 77

83

decimate populations of abalone, sea urchins, lobster, and other valuable marine resources. This faction points to documented decreases in legal-sized abalones, pismo clams, and sea urchins in central California where sea otters exist.

The 1987 translocation involved transporting 69 sea otters by air from the parent colony of 1,200 in central California. Wildlife biologists plan to collect additional animals each year for five years until 250 otters have been translocated. They are hopeful that a new breeding colony will become established at the island, helping to ensure survival of sea otters in California. Conservationists, fishermen, and divers are watching the translocation closely.

Plate 78.
Canopies are frequented by many species of birds that pick through the surface foliage looking for food. This Xantus' murrelet, *Endomychura hypopleuca*, is seen swimming in a canopy off the San Benitos Islands, Baja California, Mexico.

Plate 79.
An olive rockfish (*Sebastes serranoides*) and a school of blue rockfish (*Sebastes mystinus*), hang motionless beneath a canopy off Point Lobos, in central California. Schools of blue rockfish numbering in the hundreds are often seen in kelp forests, where they feed on plankton. This species is characteristic of inhabitants of the cold waters off central California and northward.

Plate 78

Plate 79

Plate 80

Elephant seals (*Mirounga angustirostris*) are a common sight in the canopies at California's San Miguel and San Nicolas Islands and at the San Benitos Islands and Cedros Island off Baja California, Mexico.

Plate 81.

A sea otter (*Enhydra lutris*) rests in a kelp canopy near Carmel Bay, California. It is common for members of this species to anchor themselves in one spot by draping fronds of the slippery kelp over their bodies. These animals forage within kelp forests, diving day and night to satisfy their appetite. After a successful dive, the otter is frequently seen lying on its back in the canopy, working industriously with a rock or other tool to open a clam or other hard-shelled animal. Some of the otter's favorite foods include crabs, sea urchins, and abalones.

Plate 80

Plate 81

Chapter 8

Santa Barbara: A Unique *Macrocystis* Environment

On a clear morning, the coastal community of Santa Barbara, California, awakens to a spectacular view of the northern Channel Islands: Anacapa, Santa Cruz, Santa Rosa, and San Miguel. Located in an almost straight line paralleling the coast, these islands serve as a barrier that lessens the brunt of bad weather that occasionally approaches Santa Barbara from the south. In addition, Point Conception, the headland of the east-west facing section of coastline of which Santa Barbara is a part, shelters the area from prevailing northwesterly ocean swells. As a result, Santa Barbara enjoys generally placid nearshore ocean conditions that allow forests of giant kelp to thrive in a unique environment—a sandy, rockless environment.

Some scientists believe that the giant kelp found off Santa Barbara is merely a form of *Macrocystis pyrifera* that has adapted to the sandy environment. Others classify it as a completely different species, *Macrocystis angustifolia*. The debate continues.

No matter what species name is used for the plants, the fact remains that it is unusual to find *Macrocystis* growing in a sand-bottom environment.

Plates 82 - 83.
Extensive forests of giant kelp have historically developed along the coast of California near Santa Barbara. This kelp is unique because it grows on sand or other soft substrate, thanks, in part, to protection from storms and swells afforded the area by the offshore Channel Islands (Plate 82).

The area offshore of the train tressle at Gaviota, California, thirty miles west of Santa Barbara, has historically been an important kelp resource (Plate 83).

Plate 82

Plate 83

The reader might wonder how a plant that relies on hard substrate for attachment in order to thrive can live in an area devoid of rocky reefs. The answer is simple. The *Macrocystis* has found a substitute for rocky reefs in the form of tube casings that house the sessile segmented marine worm species *Diopatra ornata*. This prolific worm produces a protective, leathery gray casing that is securely embedded deep into the sand. Only a small portion is visible above the ocean floor. It is that small portion that serves as substrate for the kelp.

Starting small, the kelp plant, in its microscopic stage, begins to develop on a single worm tube. As it grows, the plant sends out haptera that grasp more and more tubes. Eventually, the haptera form a massive holdfast that can cover over 100 square feet of ocean floor. During the growth process, shifting sand fills in the crevices formed by the growing haptera and also piles up around the periphery of the holdfast, helping to stabilize the plant.

The holdfasts and the many fronds that rise from them dramatically alter the underwater environment. On the average, for every 100 square feet of sandy bottom the growing kelp provides nearly 1,500 square feet of foliage and innumerable sand-filled nooks and crannies that attract a variety of animals. The holdfasts and columns of kelp are colonized by many of the same creatures common to forests on rocky reefs: encrusting bryozoans, hydroids, small crustaceans, and kelp crabs, to name a few. They live side by side with clams, cancer crabs, and other creatures that normally live on the soft sediment.

Although abundant, animals that live on the sand often go unseen. *Astropecten armatus*, a bluish-gray sea star whose body is fringed with bristling spines, often lies buried just below the surface of the sand. A star-shaped imprint reveals its presence.

A large flatfish, the California halibut (*Paralichthys californicus*), can grow to over four feet in length and

Plate 84.
Macrocystis on the soft bottom near Santa Barbara has found a substitute for rocky reefs as substrate. Juvenile plants develop on one of several kinds of tubes that protect species of segmented marine worms. This juvenile plant is developing on the tip of *Diopatra ornata*, a species of worm whose tube extends more than a foot into the soft bottom.

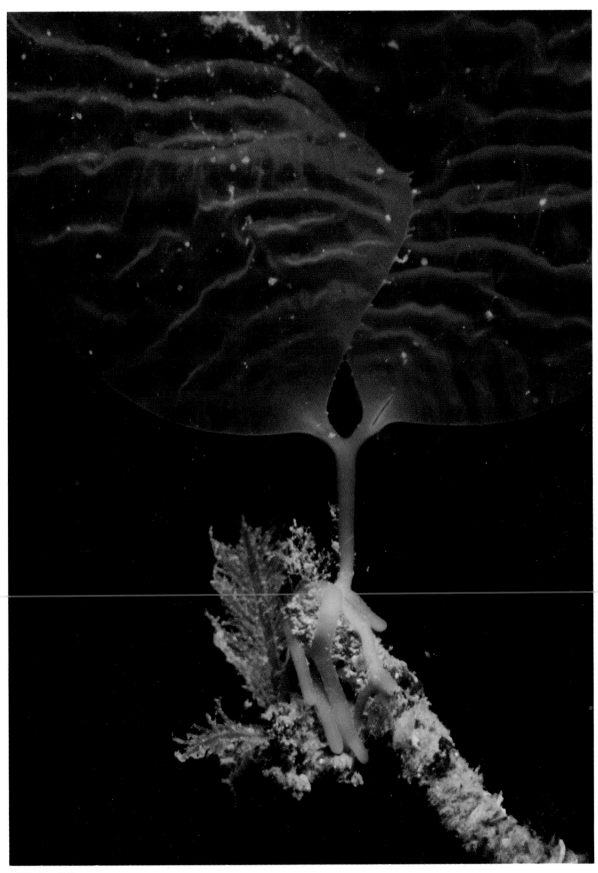

Plate 84

91

weigh over 40 pounds. While waiting for unsuspecting prey — often rockfish, surfperch, and señoritas that are attracted to the kelp environment — the halibut lies buried in the sand up to its eyeballs. When a meal comes within its reach, the halibut lunges forward, propelled by strong, rapid up-and-down sweeps of its large tail.

A smaller flatfish, the speckled sanddab (*Citharichthys stigmaeus*), can change its dorsal pattern to match the color and texture of the ocean floor. When motionless, this three- to four-inch animal becomes nearly invisible.

An unusual fish that inhabits the Santa Barbara kelp forest is the kelp pipefish (*Syngnathus californiensis*). Like its relative the sea horse, this skinny, foot-long fish has a tubular snout. The female of the species lays eggs in the male's "brood pouch," where they remain until hatched. The young pipefish emerge from the eggs as miniature, thread-sized adults. Some probably spend their entire life in the kelp bed.

Because of the typically calm ocean conditions, the giant kelp community near Santa Barbara is normally very stable, the mainstay of a vast ecosystem that changes little from year to year. Unfortunately, even the usual protection afforded by its coastline orientation and the Channel Islands barrier was not enough to protect the Santa Barbara area from the devastating El Niño that played havoc worldwide from 1982 and well into 1984. Santa Barbara was lashed by storms from the western Pacific. As in other areas, entire kelp forests were lost as whole plants were torn from their substrate and cast ashore. The few plants that did survive did not flourish during El Niño because water temperatures were high, nutrient levels low. Improved ocean conditions in recent years have resulted in renewed kelp growth, but it might be many years before the unusual kelp forests off Santa Barbara return to their pre-El Niño luxuriance.

Plates 85 - 86.
Because *Macrocystis* growing near Santa Barbara is in many ways unique, some scientists classify it as *Macrocystis angustifolia* instead of *M. pyrifera*. Sometimes, from a distance, juvenile *Macrocystis* at Santa Barbara appears to be sprouting directly from the sand. Haptera of the two-foot-high juvenile plant in Plate 85, which are attached to marine worm tube casings, are completly covered by coarse sand.

Haptera of juvenile plants that develop on worm tubes continually reach out and grasp more tubes to help secure the plant in place. Eventually the haptera form a massive holdfast (Plate 86) that can cover more than 100 square feet of ocean floor. Shifting sand fills the crevices created by the growing haptera and piles up around the edge of the holdfast. The basal portions of this plant, from which the fronds and haptera arise, are more flattened than those of typical *Macrocystis pyrifera* plants. Pink haptera can be seen growing down from the flattened basal portion of this plant (Plate 86) photographed off El Capitan State Park near Santa Barbara, California.

Plate 85

Plate 86

Plates 87 - 88.

Forests of kelp near Santa Barbara are especially unusual because they bring together animals that are typical of rocky-habitat forests and animals that live on sand. The colorful crab *Randallia ornata* (Plate 87), and the moon snail (*Polinices* sp.) in Plate 88 are two such animals typically found in sand. Here, *Randallia ornata* settles into the soft sediment. Eventually, it will cover itself completely with sand for protection from predators.

The moon snail extends its enormous white foot for locomotion. Moon snails feed primarily on clams they are able to detect hiding several inches below the surface of the sand.

Plate 87

Plate 88

Plate 89.

The speckled sanddab (*Citharichthys stigmaeus*) can change its dorsal pattern to match the color and texture of the ocean floor. It becomes nearly invisible when lying motionless and partially covered with grains of sand. The specimen shown here is approximately three inches long.

Plate 90.

A five-pound halibut (*Paralichthys californicus*), a favorite catch of fishermen who frequent the kelp beds, rests peacefully on the ocean floor as the seastar *Astropecten armatus* approaches. *Astropecten* uses its pointed "feet" for locomotion over the soft ocean floor. Its rock-dwelling relatives have feet equipped with suction cup-like tips that enable them to hold on to solid surfaces.

Plate 89

Plate 90

97

Chapter 9

The Impact
of Animals
on the Forest

Many species of animals feed on giant kelp, causing little or no damage to the plants on which they depend for nourishment. Sometimes, however, these same animals graze the plants to death.

Opaleye (*Girella nigricans*) and halfmoon perch (*Medialuna californiensis*) are fishes that feed on giant kelp, nibbling on both juvenile and adult plants. On rare occasions, these fishes are so abundant that their grazing becomes destructive. Rockfish, kelp bass, and kelp surfperch, on the other hand, are among the twenty or so fish species that help protect the forest by eating potentially destructive kelp isopods such as *Idotea resecata*. Slender, an inch and a half long, and equipped with recurved legs, these kelp isopods can usually be spotted clinging to the stipes of *Macrocystis* fronds. Left unchecked — as when their natural predators are absent or present in small numbers — these isopods multiply rapidly. Soon they scurry over giant kelp by the thousands, munching incessantly and leaving a trail of over-grazed, dying plants.

Plates 91 - 92.
Opaleye, *Girella nigricans*, are omnivorous fishes that eat kelp as well as many animals that inhabit the forest (Plate 91).

Idotea resecata (Plate 92) lives on *Macrocystis* and other species of seaweed. In 1979, hundreds of thousands of these grazing animals destroyed more than 100 acres of their kelp forest habitat off San Nicolas Island, California.

Plate 91

Plate 92

Even more destructive than kelp isopods are sea urchins. The three common urchin species found in the kelp forest are the red (*Strongylocentrotus franciscanus*), purple (*Strongylocentrotus purpuratus*), and white (*Lytechinus anamesus*).

Although related to sea stars, these voracious creatures are unique in appearance. They have round, brittle shells, or tests, that are covered with sharp, constantly moving spines. The spines serve as protective armor, assist in locomotion, and help the urchins trap food. Extending from between the spines are suction cup-tipped appendages called tube feet and pincer-tipped grabbing structures called pedicellariae. At the base of the test, in the center, is the urchin's chewing apparatus, Aristotle's lantern.

The largest of the urchins is the softball-sized red urchin. The smallest, not much larger than a ping-pong ball, is the white urchin.

Purple and red urchins usually live in rocky habitats on the forest floor, tucked away in crevices and under ledges. They also occur in small holes or pockets created by years of grinding their chewing apparatus and spines on the rocky reef surfaces where they live. While the white urchin is also found in rocky areas, it prefers sand- or silt-covered areas from shallow water to depths of several thousand feet.

All three species are well adapted for feeding on pieces of *Macrocystis* that drift within their reach. The tube feet and pedicellariae enable the urchin to grab morsels of the "drift kelp." Then, working with the spines, they pass the kelp to the chewing apparatus at the base of the animal's test.

A lush, healthy forest produces enough drift kelp to keep even large urchin populations satiated. However, when growing conditions are poor and drift kelp becomes scarce, the usually sedentary sea urchins leave

Plates 93 - 94.

The purple sea urchin, *Strongylocentrotus purpuratus* (Plate 93), is one of three species common in forests of giant kelp off California and Baja California, Mexico. The others are the red, *Strongylocentrotus franciscanus*, and the white, *Lytechinus anamesus*, sea urchins.

All sea urchins have a brittle shell or test that is covered with sharp spines, suction cup-tipped tube feet, and pincer-like grabbing structures called pedicellariae, as shown here in Plate 93.

The sea urchin's chewing appartus is located on the underside of the test. Five white teeth, part of a complex feeding structure called Aristotle's lantern, are clearly visible on the red sea urchin in Plate 94.

Plate 93

Plate 94

their protective surroundings in search of food: microscopic algae, seaweeds, and of course, giant kelp. Grazing urchins attack the holdfasts of giant kelp plants, severing fronds at their base. The severed fronds, made buoyant by their numerous pneumatocysts, simply float to the surface and drift away. This waste of food increases the number of plants that must be attacked in order to sustain the urchins.

Occasionally, sea urchins travel across the forest floor in vast swarms. Like locusts, they strip all vegetation from areas in their path. Dense urchin aggregations, referred to as feeding fronts by scientists, can level a forest at the rate of 30 feet per month. After a feeding front passes, urchin densities in a given area decline. But enough urchins usually remain to prevent kelp regrowth.

Areas that are completely devoid of kelp due to grazing by the urchin population are called "barrens." Research has shown that urchin larvae frequently settle in barrens in large numbers. This massive "recruitment" helps to ensure the perpetuation of the barrens.

Urchin grazing can be halted or reduced, enabling re-establishment of kelp forests in decimated areas. Disease sometimes causes die-offs of entire urchin communities. Predation by the sheephead, California spiny lobster, sea otter, and even humans helps keep the urchin population in check. The best example of the effect of predation is found in kelp forests frequented by otters. In such forests, large urchin populations do not exist, so the potential for over-grazing is minimal. Off Monterey, California, an increased sea otter population is credited with reducing the number of urchins to such an extent that once sparse kelp beds flourish today.

When the poor weather or water quality conditions that ultimately lead to an urchin feeding frenzy are replaced by near perfect conditions, kelp beds outside the barrens once again become lush. Fast growing plants

Plate 95.
Sea urchins typically live tucked beneath protective rocky ledges and feed on pieces of *Macrocystis* and other seaweeds that drift down upon them. However, when sea urchins become too numerous or drift kelp becomes scarce due to poor growing conditions, the urchins leave their protective surroundings to search for food. Here, a horde of hungry purple and red sea urchins is attacking the holdfast and fronds of a kelp plant. In time, all fronds on this *Macrocystis* plant, photographed off Point Loma, in California, will be severed by the grazing urchins and set adrift.

Plate 95

mean an increased supply of drift kelp and elimination of the need for urchins to graze. Unfortunately, it can take years for nature to run its course and return giant kelp forests to once barren areas. Researchers constantly seek improved methods of hastening the process.

Plates 96 - 97.

White tracks left in a pink crust of coralline algae tell divers and researchers that hungry urchins have been at work, scraping the ocean floor for any source of nourishment (Plate 96).

At San Nicolas Island, off southern California, voracious purple sea urchins turned a once lushly forested submarine area into an urchin barrens in 1979 (Plate 97). Unless this urchin population is checked, new generations of this animal will continue to perpetuate the barrens.

Plate 96

Plate 97

Part III

Mankind and the Forest

Plate 98.
A diver swims among towering fronds of *Macrocystis*.

Plate 98

Chapter 10

Harvesting California's Kelp Forests

As early as the 1600s, kelp was recognized in Europe as a source of potash, a potassium-rich compound used as fertilizer. But with the discovery of rich deposits of potash salts in Germany in the middle of the 19th century, most nations turned to that country for their potash needs. The United States was no exception, importing approximately 20 percent of the total output of the German potash mines annually.

In 1910, a highly publicized dispute between American importers of potash and the Kali Syndikat, the government-controlled German marketing syndicate, pointed out the extent to which the United States had grown dependent upon Germany as its source of potash for fertilizer. Such dependency was deemed dangerous by both the American public and the government. As a result, efforts were made to find an alternate source of potash at home. Kelp seemed a perfect choice.

By 1913, several small kelp-harvesting firms had been established in California, and kelp was being examined as a large-scale source of potash as well as

Plates 99 - 100.

Kelp harvesting has undergone major changes since the 1920s.

The *Pinole* (Plate 99) was one of the early vessels used by Kelco Company, which began harvesting giant kelp near San Diego, California, in 1929. Operating from the deck of the *Pinole*, workers gathered kelp using long poles with hooks on the end. Once the kelp was drawn alongside the vessel, it was cut and pulled aboard. Six men working all day could collect fifty tons of giant kelp in this manner.

The *El Capitan* (Plate 100) was one of the first mechanical harvesters built by Kelco. Completed in 1941, it had a capacity of nearly 300 tons and could venture to kelp beds as far away as Santa Barbara, 180 miles northwest of San Diego. Two large cutting racks with reciprocating blades mounted at the base of a conveyor system were secured to the vessel's bow. These were lowered into the water to a depth of four feet during harvesting. Cut kelp was brought aboard by the conveyor and deposited in the kelp bin that made up most of the vessel.

Plate 99

Plate 100

other by-products that could be sold to help make harvesting and processing kelp a profitable venture.

The outbreak of hostilities in Europe led to an embargo on the export of German-mined potash salts. It also led to an increased demand for potash and acetone to be used in the manufacture of gunpowder for American soldiers and their allies.

Kelp became big business. Harvesting companies flourished. The Hercules Powder Company of San Diego was the largest and most successful of eleven California-based kelp companies during the war, reportedly employing 1500 people in its prime.

The signing of the Armistice in November 1918, in addition to signaling the end of the war, also signaled the beginning of the end for the early California kelp industry. A drastic drop in the price of potash, coupled with the cancellation of government explosives contracts, led to the virtual collapse of commercial harvesting by 1919.

The eventual rebirth of the California kelp industry in the late 1920s was the result of a discovery made nearly half a century earlier by British chemist E.C.C. Stanford. In 1883, Stanford described algin, a unique substance found in the cell walls of kelp. It is algin that accounts for kelp's extreme flexibility and enables the plant to withstand the forces of surf and surge. Combined with fluids containing water, algin has the ability to control their flow characteristics.

The world's first producer of algin products, Kelco Company of San Diego, began as a cottage industry in 1929. That company, now a division of Merck & Co., Inc., has harvested and processed kelp ever since. It is currently the only company in the United States that harvests giant kelp for the purpose of extracting algin.

Initially, Kelco produced kelp meal, a type of livestock feed, in addition to extracting algin for use in controlling the viscosity of a gasket compound utilized

Plates 101 - 103.
By 1957, kelp harvesters at Kelco took on a sleek, modern look. The *Kelstar* (Plate 101), built in 1977, is typical of the new style.

Drapers, conveyors with reciprocating blades for cutting mounted on the base (Plate 102), are located at the stern of the modern kelp harvester. As the harvester moves stern-first through the water, kelp is cut and then held in place on the drapers until it is conveyed to the kelp bin (Plate 103).

From the wheelhouse, located directly above the drapers (Plate 103), the vessel's captain has an excellent vantage point from which to watch the harvesting operation.

Plate 101

Plate 102

Plate 103

in sealing tin cans. By 1940, the production of kelp meal was discontinued. But through continued research, the company has developed many additonal applications for algin. Today, this amazing product serves as a thickening, stabilizing, and smoothing agent in hundreds of products ranging from salad dressings to cosmetics, dental impression compounds to antacid formulations, canned foods to beer. Algin improves texture and retains moisture in bakery products. In frozen foods, its stabilizing properties assure smooth texture and uniform thawing.

Giant kelp is especially suitable for commercial use because the surface canopy can be harvested several times a year without disturbing the submerged parts of the plant, where vegetative growth and reproduction occur. The surface canopy is continually regenerated by the rapid growth of young fronds.

Harvesting methods have come a long way since the days of simply collecting kelp litter that washed ashore after storms. As late as the 1930s, one common practice involved snaring the kelp fronds with a device that resembled a gigantic crochet hook. Once snared, the kelp was cut by hand and hauled aboard a boat or barge for transport to land.

Today, kelp is harvested by large vessels that operate like seagoing versions of the wheat harvesters used by land-based farmers. En route to the kelp bed, a harvester looks and functions like most large ships. Once at its destination, however, it undergoes an amazing transformation. Large cutting racks — reciprocating blades mounted at the base of a conveyor system — are lowered from the stern of the vessel into the water to a depth of not more than four feet. Main engines are secured, and a bow propeller pushes the vessel, stern first, through the water.

Once the reciprocating blades have cut the kelp, loose fronds are prevented from floating away by vertically

Plate 104.
Kelp canopies in this aerial photo, taken with color infrared film, show up as yellow against a background of green water. The oblique photo of the Point Loma kelp bed off San Diego, California, shows kelp canopies extending from the lower left to upper right of the frame. Breaking waves with land nearby are visible on the right. Harvest tracks, in the outer half of the kelp bed, are visible running the entire length of the bed. Kelp plants to the right of the harvest tracks, cut a few weeks earlier, are already beginning to form new canopies. This kind of rapid regrowth only occurs when nutrients and sunlight are plentiful and water temperatures are cool.

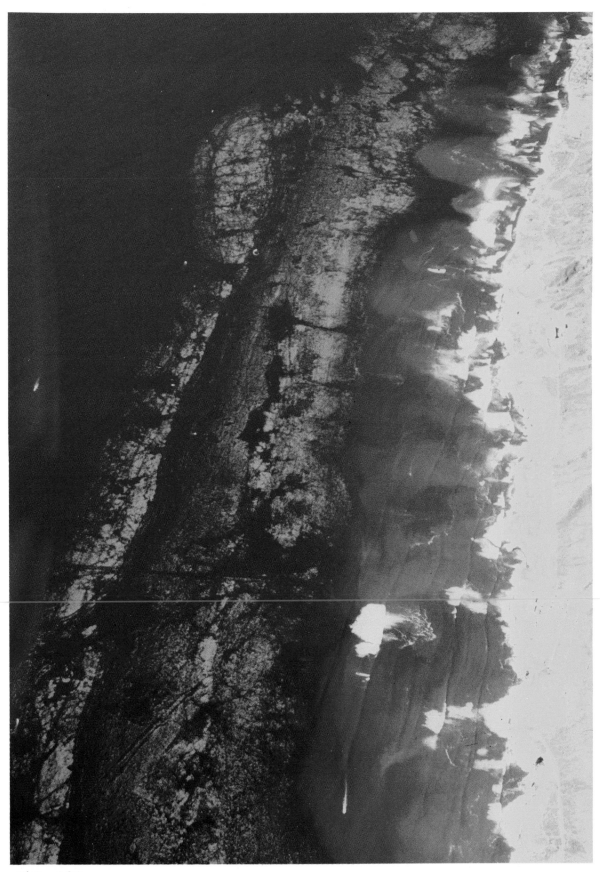

Plate 104

rotating, toothed rollers. Guided by the rollers, the fronds then begin their journey up the conveyor system and into a large bin that accounts for most of the harvester's length.

Depending on the density of the kelp bed scheduled for harvesting and the size of the vessel, up to 600 tons of kelp can be gathered in eight hours.

Regulations governing kelp harvesting have been in existence since 1917. *Macrocystis* is harvested from kelp beds leased for a period of 20 years. No one company may hold an exclusive lease on more than 25 square miles, or fifty percent of the kelp bed area, whichever is greater. The lessee pays a minimum annual fee per area leased, plus a fee per ton of kelp harvested. In addition to the leased kelp beds, there are designated "open" areas that may be harvested by any company with a kelp harvesting permit. All harvesting must take place at a depth no greater than four feet below the ocean surface.

Currently, the California Department of Fish and Game regulates kelp harvesting within California's coastal waters.

Plate 105.
A large rake with four-foot-long tines is used to evenly distribute a load of newly harvested kelp in the harvester's kelp bin. An operator in the winch house uses levers and pedals to control the rake, or "drag line."

Plate 106.
Just-harvested kelp is brought daily to Kelco's processing facility on San Diego Bay when crops are plentiful. The kelp is unloaded using a crane that can handle up to three tons of seaweed per lift. Once unloaded, the kelp is chopped, cooked, and further processed to yield algin, a natural compound that is added to many foods and other items the general public uses regularly.

Plate 105

Plate 106

Plates 107 - 109.
Algin, a natural compound found in the cell walls of giant kelp, serves as a thickening, stabilizing, and smoothing agent in hundreds of products ranging from salad dressings to cosmetics, dental impression compounds to antacid formulations, canned foods to beer (Plate 107). Algin improves texture and retains moisture in many dessert products (Plate 108). In frozen foods, its stabilizing properties assure smooth texture and uniform thawing. The primary industrial applications of algin products are paper coating and sizing, textile printing (Plate 109), and welding-rod coating.

Plate 107

Plate 108

Plate 109

Chapter 11

Fishing and Diving

The richness of life in the Amber Forest attracts fishermen, divers, photographers, naturalists, and sightseers alike. Some make a living in the forest while others are drawn there strictly for recreational pursuits.

For centuries, people have turned to animals associated with the forest for food. A mainstay of the Chumash Indian diet was abalone, a single-shelled mollusc that clings tenaciously to rocky reefs using its large, muscular "foot." The Indians harvested abalone from shallow waters inshore of the kelp beds. After dislodging the animal from its home on the reef, the Chumash would remove, tenderize, and eat the foot. They fashioned the beautiful shell into jewelry, fishing hooks, and even money. Large shells were sometimes transformed into bowls.

Thousands of years after the Chumash harvested abalone from the shoreline, Chinese immigrants established the first commercial abalone fishery in California. They learned of the abundance and marketability of abalone

Plates 110 - 111.

For centuries, people have harvested the red abalone (*Haliotis rufescens*) and other animals associated with the kelp forest for food. The seven-inch red abalone in Plate 110, with its black tentacles and mantle extended, crawls slowly over the surface of a rock covered with pink encrusting coralline algae. Today, the increasingly scarce abalone is an expensive treat in seafood restaurants.

Chumash Indians who settled along the Pacific coast as long as 10,000 years ago fashioned abalone shells into jewelry and fish hooks and even used them as money. Large shells, similar in size to the one shown in Plate 111, were sometimes used as bowls.

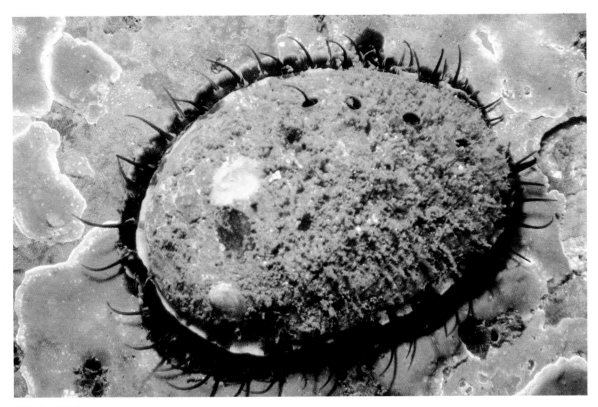

Plate 110

Plate 111

119

shortly after arriving in California to work on the railroads in the mid-1800s. Like the Chumash Indians, the Chinese began collecting abalone in shallow water along the shore. In time, as shallow-water harvesting grounds became depleted, the fishery moved into slightly deeper water. Working from skiffs, the Chinese used long, hooked poles to pry the animals from the rocks.

By the late 1800s, the Japanese established themselves as expert abalone harvesters. Forced by supply and demand into ever deeper waters, the Japanese dived into the kelp beds to search for abalone. First they "free dived," holding their breath as they worked underwater. Later they used "hard hat" gear. While cumbersome, hard hat diving enabled the divers to spend more time underwater and thus harvest more abalone.

In the late 1950s, abalone harvesters began using the "hookah" system of diving in which a boat-mounted low-pressure compressor feeds air to the diver through a lightweight hose. While similar to hard hat diving, hookah introduced several changes that made diving less cumbersome. A small face mask and a "regulator" that is held in the diver's mouth replaced the heavy hard hat helmet. Fins replaced weighted boots; dive suits were streamlined. This system, its gear updated over the years, is still used by abalone harvesters.

Strict regulations govern the harvesting of abalone in California. Species size limits are enforced, restricted numbers of commercial harvesting permits are issued, and entire areas are occasionally closed to harvesting to help manage the resource. In addition, a special tool commonly referred to as an "ab iron," must be used by harvesters. This tool has blunt edges designed to protect both the animals that successfully resist being pried from their place on the rocky reef and those that must be returned to the rocks because they are not within legal size limits.

Plate 112.
Japanese "free divers" began harvesting abalone in California during the late 1800s. Later they began to use "hard hat" gear as seen in this photo. At its height, the Japanese abalone diving fleet at Point Lobos numbered 18 vessels.

Plate 112

Of the eight species of abalone found in California, four are commercially important. The red abalone (*Haliotis rufescens*) is the most prized because of its size. Animals of this species can grow to more than eleven inches in diameter.

Another commercially important animal is the California spiny lobster (*Panulirus interruptus*). A shy creature, the spiny lobster generally hides in caves and crevices during the day, venturing forth at night to scavenge for food. Unlike the Maine lobster, the California lobster has no claws. Instead it is armed with protective spines.

The spiny lobster fishery developed in Santa Barbara over a century ago. It quickly spread to Los Angeles and San Diego. Today, lobsters are trapped from Santa Barbara County in California to central Baja California, Mexico.

During lobster season, which runs from early October through mid-March in California, kelp canopies are speckled with colorful buoys. The buoys, which carry the lobster fishermen's permit numbers, are tethered to traps that rest on the ocean floor. The typical lobster trap is a wire-mesh cage with two funnel-shaped side openings. It is baited with dead fish to attract the scavenging lobsters. Once a lobster enters the trap, its long antennae, five pairs of gangly walking legs, and spines prevent it from escaping through the small end of the funnel.

At first light, lobster fishermen prepare their skiffs and travel to the kelp forest, zigzagging through the canopies as they retrieve trap after trap. Captured lobsters are checked to see if they are of legal size. The hard carapace, that part of the body from just behind the eyes to the beginning of the tail, must measure 3 1/4 inches or more in length. "Shorts" must be returned to the sea. It usually takes ten years for a lobster to reach legal size. Still, after all those years of growth, the animal usually weighs less than a pound.

Plate 113.
The California spiny lobster (*Panulirus interruptus*) occurs from Point Conception, California down through Baja California, Mexico. This crustacean is prized by sport divers and commercial fishermen alike. A shy creature, the spiny lobster usually hides in caves and crevices by day, venturing forth at night to search for food.

Sportdivers, using scuba or free-diving with a mask and fins, capture spiny lobsters in rocky reefs near forests of giant kelp. By law, the divers in California may use only their hands to catch the quick crustaceans. The animals are so difficult to catch by hand that usually only the experienced diver does well on a lobster dive.

Commercial lobster fishermen in California set wire-mesh traps during the season, which lasts from early October through mid-March. During that period, kelp canopies are speckled with colorful buoys tethered to traps below. The traps are usually baited with dead fish, which attracts the lobster during its nightly walk.

Plate 113

A second spiny creature, the prolific red sea urchin, is the foundation of a lucrative west coast fishery. Urchin sex organs, or roe, are considered a delicacy in Japan, where they are called "uni." Because of the popularity of uni both in Japan and in Japanese sushi restaurants located in other countries, demand for and commercial take of the softball-sized urchins has skyrocketed in recent years. Divers harvested a modest 200 pounds of red urchins in 1971, the fishery's first year. In 1986, they bagged an extraordinary 30 million pounds. Most of the roe is earmarked for shipment to Japan.

Using hookah gear, divers search the kelp beds for dense concentrations of sea urchins. Once a population is located, a few of the animals are cracked open to check the quality of the roe. Buyers prefer yellow or bright orange roe that is about two inches long. Using a short-handled rake, an experienced diver can harvest over 2,000 pounds of urchins per day. Although sold salted, steamed, baked, or frozen, uncooked fresh urchin roe is preferred by gourmets.

Japanese gourmet preferences have not only inspired California's burgeoning sea urchin fishery, they are also responsible for "spawn-on-kelp," an unusual fishery developed in Alaska and British Columbia over a decade ago and recently introduced in the San Francisco Bay area. This fishery is based on the spawning behavior of Pacific herring (*Clupea harengus*) that gather by the millions each spring to lay their eggs in bays from Alaska to California. The herring deposit their sticky eggs, a prized delicacy known as "kazunoko," on almost anything, including many species of seaweed.

Herring eggs deposited on blades of giant kelp are preferred by true kazunoko connoisseurs and thus command a high price. Therefore, ingenious fishermen have developed methods to ensure that the herring lay their eggs specifically on *Macrocystis*. Because the fish

Plates 114 - 115.

A load of harvested sea urchins (Plate 114), taken from the kelp forests off San Clemente Island by the crew of a Santa Barbara-based vessel, is destined for Japanese markets. In Japan, sea urchin sex organs, or roe (Plate 115), are considered a delicacy.

Divers collect only healthy red urchins larger than two and a half inches in diameter. These urchins, which thrive on a diet of *Macrocystis*, develop yellow or bright orange roe, the color discriminating buyers prefer.

The vessel in Plate 114 will transport its harvest to a pick-up boat that waits in a nearby cove. The pick-up boat, after collecting urchins from several boats, will hurry the sea creatures to the mainland for processing.

Plate 114

Plate 115

generally spawn in areas where giant kelp does not grow naturally, the fishermen collect or import fronds and suspend them from large, floating racks. Some fishermen simply maneuver these structures over the spawning fish. Others enclose the structures with mesh, creating herring pounds. Once spawning begins, it takes only a few hours for the fish to blanket the blades of kelp with eggs. To ensure freshness, the egg-laden blades are immediately collected, packed in brine, and shipped to sushi restaurants throughout the world. The spawn-on-kelp is served sliced into thin morsels that contain a strip of giant kelp sandwiched between layers of eggs.

A very controversial commercial fishing technique is gill netting. While fishing with a hook and line is challenging and exhilarating, it is not very productive in terms of pounds caught per day. Gill netting, on the other hand, is designed to catch many marketable fish in little time. This helps make commercial fishing a profitable venture and keeps the price of fresh fish reasonably low.

The fish sought in the kelp beds by gill net fishermen is the highly prized white seabass. When fish of this species venture into the kelp forest to rest or search for food, they become hopelessly entangled in the net, which hangs from surface buoys like a huge mesh curtain. The controversy over this fishing method stems from the fact that non-target animals, including marine mammals such as seals, sea lions, and even an occasional gray whale, sometimes become ensnared and die in the nets.

Sportfishermen, like their commercial counterparts, are drawn to forests of giant kelp. Large charter boats and smaller private vessels frequently line the edge of a kelp bed as those on board try to land kelp bass, rockfish, or other fishes that live among the fronds. Bent rods, a flurry of activity, and joyful shouts mean that fishing is good.

Those who dive in the kelp beds soon develop a special appreciation for the creatures that live there. Some

Plate 116.
Japanese gourmet preferences have inspired the "spawn-on-kelp" fishery in Alaska and British Columbia, Canada. The fishery is based on the spawning behavior of Pacific herring (*Clupea harengus*) that gather by the millions each spring to lay their eggs. The herring deposit their sticky white eggs, a prized delicacy known as "kazunoko," on almost anything, including fronds of giant kelp.

This photo shows a purse sein boat, used for catching the herring, tied to the holding pens. Blades of giant kelp in the foreground have a light cover of herring eggs deposited on them.

Plate 116

divers descend into the forest in search of game. Others prefer sightseeing or photography. In recent years, sophisticated underwater camera equipment has enabled novice as well as professional photographers to capture life in the forest on film. Photos taken by diving photographers, when shared with others, help develop an understanding of the complex kelp bed ecosystem.

Plate 117.
Divers can venture past the shore and into kelp forests such as this one off the Monterey Peninsula in California.

Plate 117

Chapter 12

Conservation and Education

British naturalist and explorer Charles Darwin was among the first to recognize the importance of forests of giant kelp as a habitat for many creatures. Based on observations he made during the famous voyage of the *HMS Beagle* in 1834, Darwin noted:

> *The number of living creatures of all Orders, whose existence intimately depends on the kelp, is wonderful. A great volume might be written, describing the inhabitants of one of these beds of seaweed... I can only compare these great aquatic forests with the terrestrial ones in the intertropical regions. Yet, if in any country a forest was destroyed, I do not believe nearly so many species of animals would perish as would here, from the destruction of the kelp.*

Darwin's appreciation of and concern for forests of *Macrocystis* have long been shared by naturalists and scientists. In recent years, thanks to museum and aquarium exhibits featuring the giant seaweed, the general public has been exposed to the importance and uniqueness of this phenomenal plant.

Plate 118.

A marine biologist, using a video camera, swims through a kelp forest to record the swaying plants that surround him. He is one of many researchers who, outfitted in the latest scuba equipment, including a comfortable, insulating drysuit, studies the dynamics of the undersea forests. Biologists use a plethora of paraphernalia in addition to video cameras to measure and document the kelp forest habitat. The unsuspecting sportdiver is often surprised to find permanent markings that outline submarine study plots or *Macrocystis* fronds flagged with bright pink surveyor's tape.

Plate 118

In 1910, studies initiated by the California Fish and Game Commission, Scripps Institution of Oceanography, the United States Bureau of Soils, and the United States Bureau of Fisheries provided a basis for kelp harvesting practices and regulations that has endured over the years. However, after the first flurry of extensive investigation, interest in kelp bed research diminished until the 1950s, when valued kelp beds in the San Diego and Los Angeles metropolitan areas began to deteriorate. In response to the problem, studies designed to identify the causes of deterioration and to devise means to reverse the destructive trend were undertaken.

Pollution was cited as the major contributor to the destruction of the kelp forests. Researchers determined that effluents containing human and industrial waste products increased water turbidity, which, in turn, diminished the quantity and quality of light available to the kelp for growth-producing photosynthesis. To make matters worse, settling waste products buried microscopic plants before they could become established. Researchers also noted that the harvesting of sheephead and lobsters, natural enemies of the sea urchin, contributed to the problem. Unchecked, increased urchin populations led to "feeding fronts" that consumed the few plants that were able to withstand the effects of pollution.

Among the techniques scientists developed to restore deteriorating kelp beds were the use of quicklime (calcium oxide) to reduce urchin populations and the transplantation of healthy kelp plants to devastated areas. In addition, improved waste treatment procedures and more stringent waste discharge regulations intended to reduce pollution were introduced.

The reduction of urchin populations, transplantation of giant kelp, and improved pollution controls helped increase canopies off Point Loma from a mere 60 acres in 1963 to 2,000 acres in 1987. Off Palos Verdes, where

Plates 119 - 120.

Purple and white sea urchins are presently being controlled by Kelco divers at specific sites in the Point Loma, California kelp bed. Sea urchins that are present even in moderate numbers can prevent giant kelp and other species of seaweed from developing.

Plate 119 shows the type of area presently being worked by divers using dredges or hammers to reduce the urchin population. Once the sea urchins are removed, tiny spores of *Macrocystis* and other seaweeds settle and begin to develop. Within a few months the bottom is carpeted with juvenile plants.

A dense, young kelp forest developed at Point Loma (Plate 120), in 1987, following a sea urchin removal project by Kelco. The urchin removal was accomplished during February and March of the year. Within eight months, young *Macrocystis* plants grew to the surface and began to produce canopy. This photo, taken during late September 1987, shows kelp bass (*Paralabrax clathratus*) and black surfperch (*Embiotoca jacksoni*) that are making this "new" forest their home.

Plate 119

Plate 120

133

only two kelp plants remained in 1967, the canopy covered over 1,000 acres in 1987.

Currently, several new kelp bed restoration techniques are being pioneered in the sand-bottom environment off Santa Barbara, where beds of giant kelp were destroyed by severe storms spawned by the 1982-84 El Niño. This work, funded by a $200,000 grant from the California Department of Fish and Game, is being done by marine biologists from Kelco. One technique involves transplanting juvenile *Macrocystis* to weighted chain link structures that are placed in rows on the ocean floor. If the project goes according to plan, the structurers will become overgrown with *Macrocystis*. In time, the chain link will deteriorate and disappear, leaving behind a flourishing submarine forest.

In addition to the efforts of scientists to preserve forests of giant kelp, many west coast aquariums, museums, and parks are working to educate the general public about the kelp bed ecosystem through special exhibits and aquarium displays. At the Channel Islands National Park, located off the coast of California, visitors can participate in an unusual summer interpretive program that involves sending a diver armed with a video camera into the kelp forest that surrounds Anacapa Island. On land, participants in the program see what the diver is seeing via monitors in a special seaside viewing area. They are also in voice contact with the diver, who is able to answer questions about the kelp bed and its inhabitants.

The Monterey Bay Aquarium in Monterey, California, has undertaken what is undoubtedly the most ambitious attempt to date to display the kelp bed habitat in a manmade setting. In a huge aquarium tank that contains over 300,000 gallons of seawater, a growing kelp forest thrives. In it are fishes, anemones, snails, crabs, and other creatures found naturally in submarine forests. This display gives divers and non-divers alike an opportunity

Plates 121 - 122.
New restoration techniques are being pioneered to re-establish giant kelp to the sand-bottom environment near Santa Barbara, California.

One technique involves using sections of weighted chain link fencing as a substrate to attach juvenile plants. In Plate 121, a biologist inspects one of the substrates prior to its use in the ocean.

The young plants seen in Plate 122 were banded to pieces of tubing and fastened to the chain link material. As the plants grow over the fence material, their holdfasts become secured to the bottom. Within a year, the plants will enlarge, produce numerous fronds, and develop a surface canopy.

Plate 121

Plate 122

to see mature plants that soar 28 feet to the tank's surface as well as juvenile plants in their various stages of development.

Innovative programs such as those at Anacapa Island and the Monterey Bay Aquarium enable the general public to join researchers in better understanding the role of kelp and the kelp bed environment in modern day living. Such programs also make people more aware of the importance of preserving this valuable resource we call **The Amber Forest**.

Plate 123.

Scientists continue to learn about forests of giant kelp through monitoring programs and specific research projects. Here, a researcher, propelled by a battery-powered diving vehicle, surveys a kelp forest. She can cover several times more distance on a single tank of air using the diving vehicle than she could swimming.

Plate 124.

A kelp forest habitat, complete with invertebrates and fishes, thrives in a huge, 300,000-gallon tank at the Monterey Bay Aquarium in Monterey, California. This exhibit is one of many efforts by aquariums, museums, and parks on the west coast to educate the general public about the kelp forest ecosystem.

Plate 123

Plate 124

Plate 125.
Canopies of giant kelp rest on a quiet sea off Point Lobos State Reserve, near Carmel, California.

Plate 125

Glossary

Algae
Plants of simple structure. Nearly all are marine or freshwater. They range in size from microscopic to more than 200 feet in length.

Algin
A natural substance found in the cell walls of kelp plants. When mixed with substances containing water, this unique substance controls their flow characteristics.

Amphipods
Small shrimp-like crustaceans that are compressed from side to side. The legs of these animals are used for walking and swimming. The name (a compound of "amphi," which means "both," and "poda," which means "feet") is derived from the animals' legs, which are used for both walking and swimming. Amphipods range in size from near microscopic to more than an inch.

Apical Blade
A specialized blade at the tip of a growing *Macrocystis* frond. Regular blades with bladders attached initiate and develop from the apical blade.

Bryozoans
A group of animals commonly called moss animals. These animals, of which there are approximately 4,000 species worldwide, are usually colonial, producing encrusting or upright colonies of hundreds of individuals. The individuals of the colony are usually less than 1/50 inch in length. Colonies are extremely variable in size and shape.

Canopy
The upper foliage of the kelp forest that frequently shades the environment below. Giant kelp produces dense canopy at the surface of the ocean.

Carapace
A hard dorsal shield that covers various species of animals, including lobsters, crabs, and shrimps.

Crustaceans
A class of animals that includes crabs, shrimps, lobsters, barnacles, and many smaller shrimp-like animals. They range in size from microscopic to several feet long. All contain an external skeleton that is shed during growth.

Detritus
Dead organic tissue and the live microorganisms that decompose this material.

Dorsal
Pertaining to the back of an animal.

Echolocation
A technique used by whales and porpoises to navigate and locate prey by releasing sound waves.

Filter Feeders
Animals that filter food from the surrounding water using a variety of specialized structures.

Fronds

The "shoots" of giant kelp that eventually grow to the surface. These structures consist of a stem-like portion (stipe) and leaf-like blades with attached bladders that provide floation.

Gametes

Eggs and sperm.

Gametophytes

The gamete-producing generation in plants. In *Macrocystis*, the gametophyte generation is the microsopic phase of the life cycle. These tiny plants produce gametes — eggs and sperm.

Haptera

Branching strands that are root-like in appearance. These structures securely anchor kelp plants to the substrate.

Holdfast

An attachment organ that firmly secures kelp plants to the substrate. Haptera make up this structure.

Hookah

A diving system that uses a lightweight hose to feed air to a submerged diver from a low-pressure compressor located above water.

Hydroids

Generally speaking, small, colonial animals that are tree-like in form. Most hydroids consist of many polyps with tentacles that surround a small mouth. Hydroids are related to corals, sea anemones, and jellyfish.

Isopods

Shrimp-like animals that are flattened from top to bottom. They usually have legs of equal size. It is from this characteristic that their name is derived: "iso" means "equal" and "pod" means "leg" or "foot." Most isopods range in size from 1/8 inch to about two inches.

Leviathan

A large and powerful aquatic animal mentioned in passages of the *Scripture*. The term commonly refers to whales.

Mollusc

A major group (phylum) of animals that includes clams, snails, sea slugs, and octopuses. Mollusca, which means "soft," refers to the soft body possessed by members of this phylum. The soft body of some molluscs is protected by an external shell.

Nudibranchs

Marine "slugs" that have variable form and are often colorful. These animals are molluscs that are related to snails but lack a shell.

Photosynthesis

The process by which plants convert carbon dioxide and water into sugar using the sun's energy.

Pinnipeds

Marine mammals whose fore and hind limbs are modified to form flippers. Seals and sea lions are members of this group.

Pneumatocysts
Gas-filled bladders that float giant kelp and other seaweeds in the water.

Potash
Potassium-rich ash produced from burning wood or kelp.

Quicklime
Calcium oxide. Quicklime reacts with sea water to produce calcium hydroxide, calcium carbonate, and heat. Research at the Scripps Institution of Oceanography led to the use of quicklime to control grazing sea urchins that were destroying kelp forests. Divers applied quicklime directly upon the sea urchins. It was the heat from the reaction with sea water that killed the destructive grazers.

Reciprocating Blades
Specialized blades on a kelp harvester. While one blade remains stationary, the other moves back and forth, cutting the kelp. These blades operate in a way similar to those of an electric hedge trimmer.

Reticular
Net-like, lacy, or intricate in appearance.

Roe
The reproductive organs and supportive tissues in sea urchins that are considered a delicacy by many.

Sessile
Pertaining to organisms that attach themselves, often for life, to the ocean floor and other substrates.

Spawning
Producing or depositing eggs.

Sporophylls
Reproductive blades on *Macrocystis* that produce spores. These narrow blades are located at the base of giant kelp, immediately above the holdfast.

Sporophyte
The spore-producing generation in giant kelp. This is the "adult" plant that eventually produces canopy.

Stipe
The stem-like portion of the giant kelp plant.

Substrate
A surface or structure to which animals and plants attach.

Test
The shell (composed of calcium carbonate) that protects the soft internal body and supports the spines of the sea urchin. The test, as well as the spines, is covered by a thin layer of tissue.

Translocation
The transfer of growth products produced by photosynthesis from one part of a plant to another. Elongate cells in the central tissues of *Macrocystis* translocate the products.

Turbidity
The state of being muddy, cloudy, not clear: as turbid water.

Photo Credits

Shane Anderson — 38, 71
Dennis Bishop — 116
Richard Bumann — 52
Marc Chamberlain — 42, 45, 67, 110, 113
Troy Delle — 63
Larry Deysher — 17
Dale A. Glantz — Cover, 1, 3, 4, 5, 7, 8, 9, 14, 15, 16, 19, 22, 25, 29, 32, 34, 35, 36, 37, 39, 49, 50, 56, 62, 69, 74, 75, 76, 77, 78, 85, 91, 93, 101, 103, 108, 109, 111, 115, 119, 120, 123
Pat Hathaway Historical Photographs — 112
Richard Herrmann — 46, 47
Kelco Division of Merck & Co., Inc. — 99, 100, 107, 121
Lovell and Libby Langstroth —79
Ken Loyst — 125
Ronald H. McPeak — 2, 6, 10, 11, 12, 13, 18, 20, 21, 23, 24, 26, 27, 28, 30, 31, 33, 40, 43, 44, 48, 51, 53, 54, 55, 57, 58, 59, 60, 61, 64, 65, 66, 68, 70, 72, 73, 80, 81, 82, 83, 84, 86, 87, 88, 89, 90, 92, 94, 96, 97, 98, 102, 104, 105, 106, 114, 117, 118, 122, Back Cover
Monterey Bay Aquarium — 124, © 1988 Monterey Bay Aquarium, All Rights Reserved
Mark Otjens — 41, 95

Selected Reading

Crandall, W. C. 1915. *Potash from Kelp: The Kelp Beds from Lower California to Puget Sound*. U.S. Dept. of Agriculture Report 100.

Daegling, M. 1986. *Monster Seaweeds: The Story of Giant Kelps*. Dillon Press, Inc.

Darwin, C. R. 1962. *The Voyage of the Beagle*. Leonard Engel, ed. New York: Doubleday.

Foster, M. S. and D. R. Schiel. 1985. *The Ecology of Giant Kelp Forests in California: A Community Profile*. U. S. Department of Interior, Fish and Wildlife Service, Biological Report 85(7.2).

North, W. J. and C. L. Hubbs. 1968. *Utilization of Kelp-Bed Resources in Southern California*. California Department of Fish and Game. California Fish and Game Bulletin, No. 139.

North, W. J. 1971. *The Biology of Giant Kelp Beds* (Macrocystis) *in California*. Nova Hedwigia: 32.

Schofield, W. L. 1959. *History of Kelp Harvesting in California*. California Department of Fish and Game. California Fish and Game, Vol. 45, no. 3.